Table of Contents

Introduction:

"¿Te cogiste a mi hija? ¿La conoces desde antes? ¡Porque ella si es una gran puta[1]!" December 17, 2023. And how do I know when this happened? Because she was arrested for *Assault Causes Bodily Injury Family Violence* against me on that date. Yeah, it's going to be that kind of story…

I used to think that a narcissistic vampire was a fictional thing – a bad guy created for a novel or a movie. But as it turns out, I found the queen of them. As a matter-of-fact, I've decided to call her "Nevdra" because it's a combination of narcissistic vampire and her real first name. It's also shorter than what she called herself at one point – *La Madre de Mentiras*[2].

So what is a narcissistic vampire you ask? Narcissistic Personality Disorder[3] is a mental disorder where a person has at least five of the following: (1) an exaggerated sense of self-importance; (2) fixation on power or beauty; (3) belief that they can only be understood by others above the rest like them; (4) need for excessive admiration; (5) sense of

---

[1] Translation: "Did you fuck my daughter? Do you know her from before? Because she's a real ho!"

[2] Translation: "The Mother of Lies"

[3] Diagnostic and Statistical Manual of Mental Disorders, Fifth Edition (DSM-5).

entitlement; (6) exploitative of others; (7) lack of empathy; (8) extreme envy; and / or (9) arrogant attitude. Basically, what people used to call a sociopath which is also what people used to call a psychopath even though those two terms have an actual definition.

"Let's Meet Up with my Friend"

How did I meet Nevdra, you ask? Well, on December 29, 2012 my best friend at the time, Cindy, hit me up as she often did to invite me out. At that point in time in my life, I was single and already a practicing lawyer. Before you get the wrong idea, you know those stereotypical lawyers who drive fancy cars, live in luxury apartments, take expensive vacations, etc? Yeah, I've never been *that* kind of lawyer. I've always been on the poorer side since I've generally worked for the government and nonprofit organizations. I guess that might help put things that happen years later in context, so just make sure that you keep that in mind when you form a construction of me as the protagonist of the story. Not the hero of the story, because I'm no hero, just the protagonist, the main character.

So, the invitation to go out wasn't anything out-of-the-ordinary. Cindy wanted to go out to a club but when it was time to go out, she asked if it was cool if we met up with one of her friends first. Cindy said that she was at a sushi place, so I was down to go get some sushi.

When we arrived, my future ex-wife was at a table with her boyfriend at the time. Since Nevdra was there with her boyfriend, I didn't look for any attraction. They were finishing up eating, so I was more disappointed than anything but I ordered something quick so that we could get that out of the way. To my surprise, her boyfriend tells us that he's going to head out and leaves Nevdra there with us. So, he takes the car (it was a nice sports car from what I remember) seemingly without any plans to come back. But everyone seemed cool with it; I thought it was kind of weird that he would leave his girl with a dude that he just met. I mean I guess that I was with her friend and maybe he thought that I was Cindy's dude, but still. Cindy and Nevdra couldn't have been that good of friends at that time because Cindy later commented to someone that she was trying to set me and Nevdra up when she introduced us but didn't know that she had a boyfriend at the time – she didn't tell me nor Nevdra that this was her intention by the way.

The three of us stayed at the Mexican sushi bar and restaurant[4] for a little bit before heading out to an actual club / bar. We hung out for a few hours and had a good time, mostly drinking and clowning around. When it was time for the place to close, Nevdra wanted to go to an after-

---

[4] Yes, that's a thing… and as you'd expect, there's a lot of spicy sushi

hours place. But, I had this really ominous feeling that something really bad would happen if I went. I couldn't shake that feeling. It was something crazy that I had never experienced before. Cindy suggested that I should follow my gut feeling and not go. But since Nevdra kept insisting that she wanted to go, Cindy suggested that I just drop them off and not go in myself. Being a gentleman, I did not like that idea. But they told me that Nevdra's boyfriend would pick them up from the club when they were done. After I confirmed this[5], I obliged them and dropped them off and went home. Cindy let me know that they made it home okay at the end of the night.

At some point I became Facebook friends with Nevdra and got her number[6]. But we talked throughout the years, mostly on Facebook or via text. Sometimes we would stop talking for years at a time. No particular reason, just life. As for seeing each other, I did attend several of her birthday parties – every time it happened to be with Cindy. Speaking of Cindy, the two times that Nevdra and I did go out, it was in a group. One time on September 14, 2014, it was with Cindy and my homeboy to a club where Cindy's daughter was celebrating her birthday. That night, Nevdra

---

[5] I think that they either showed me a text or I heard him on the phone
[6] Don't remember in which order to be honest

and I actually showed interest in each other and we kept trying to sneak off to dance together, but Cindy kept finding us and returning us to the party. But by the end of the night, my buddy was hitting on Nevdra — but she shut him down real quick. I was driving everyone home in my car and I was going to drop him off first but he asked for me to drop him off at Nevdra's place and she straight up told him "why? You don't possibly think that I'm going to sleep with you!" I laughed so hard that I almost crashed the car.

The other time we went out was actually before that on September 8, 2013. We somehow decided to go out to eat and then hit a club. After we ate[7], we went back to my place so that I could walk the dogs before we went to the next place. For some reason the electricity was off at my apartment. I was worried that Nevdra would think that it was some kind of trick, but she was cool with it. I walked the dogs while Nevdra stayed on the couch in the living room – where she started drinking my commemorative bottle of Panamanian seco. Nevdra wanted to go back to the apartment that she was living at with her friend Irene so that she could

---

[7] I don't really recall where or how that went

get changed and touch up her hair and makeup. While there, Nevdra invited Irene to go to the club with us.

At the club Irene saw a promoter that she used to hook up with and he got us into the club for free and gave us a free bottle. After a while Nevdra and I hung out without Irene since Irene went off with her old fling. But, towards the end of the night Nevdra and Irene got into some sort of argument that I thought was going to turn physical at one point. But I managed to intervene between them and dropped Nevdra off at her place. I guess that they made up the next day or so since they still lived together. When I asked for my empty bottle back (I really liked the design on it), Nevdra had told me that they threw it away to prevent Irene's son from drinking it (even though I'm sure that Nevdra finished the bottle herself after I left it there).

I did see Nevdra two other times. At some point, Nevdra had asked me for $50, so I lent it to her. I don't remember what it was for, but I think that it had something to do with a cell phone. So much time had passed that I completely forgot about it until she tells me one day "hey I haven't forgotten about the $50 you lent me; I have it and please let me get it to you before I spend it". I told Nevdra that I had forgotten about it, so don't worry about it but she insisted on paying me back. So, I went to Nevdra's apartment to pick it up. That's really all I came for. So after she gave it to me, I told Nevdra that I was going to head back now. She asked me if I didn't want to go out to eat or catch a movie or hang out somewhere, but I had just eaten before I left my place and I had work that I wanted to finish that night, so I declined. Nevdra seemed really disappointed and kept asking if I was sure. Yeah, I know… I was really naïve and innocent and didn't realize that she was just using the money as an excuse to try to get me to hang out with her.

One day Nevdra was talking to me late at night (probably drunk looking back at it) and she tells me "te tengo que decir algo[8]…" I tell her to go ahead and after a ridiculously long pause she says "me gustas[9]". She immediately hangs up on me. I text her back saying something along the lines of "Oh… I don't know, we've never even gone out on a date or anything." So, I've always found Nevdra attractive and thought that she was cool. Nevdra was always nice to me and I enjoyed talking to her. BUT, I always had a feeling that she was like a viper that would eat me alive so I never tried with her. Well, this was around September 2013 and there was a Puerto Rican festival coming up so I invited her to go with me.

---

[8] Translation: "I have to tell you something"
[9] Translation: "I like you"

I figured that it would be a chance for us to hang out together just me and her to see what was up.

So, how did that go? Well, the day of the festival, I kept trying to call and text her to see when we were going to meet up – I assumed that I was going to pick her up, but even if that was the case, I wouldn't just go to her place unless I knew for sure that she was there. I don't even think that I had her current address then.

Eventually, it's time for the festival to start so I gave up and asked my friend if she wanted to go. My friend said that she was bored and had no plans so she agreed to meet me there. While already there with my friend, Nevdra finally talks to me to let me know that she had gone out and gotten drunk the night before and just woke up. I told Nevdra that I was already there, so it was a little too late.

Maybe an hour after that, Nevdra tells me that she showed up anyway and was there with her friends. Nevdra told me that she was wearing a Puerto Rican shirt… *surprisingly* I actually did run into Nevdra there. I was still there with my friend so I introduced them, but my friend kind of walked off after that. Nevdra had a really sad look on her face and even lightly punched my chest. I never forgot the look of sadness in her eyes. I felt a little bad, but there wasn't anything that I could really do about it at that point. We parted ways and I didn't see Nevdra for the rest of the night.

I kind of stopped talking to Nevdra after that because I figured that if you have the chance to hang out with someone that you really like, then you would take it seriously and at least make an attempt to take advantage of it. So wasting her opportunity because she was hungover just showed me how unimportant I was to her and just confirmed that she wouldn't be worth attempting to date. And I had such a blast with my friend that I went to the Puerto Rican festival with, that we ended up hanging out more and more and eventually ended up dating after that.

Through the years Nevdra and I kept in contact, but outside of those times that I previously mentioned, we didn't see each other. Fast forward to Fall of 2019 with me being married with my first daughter already. Even though Nevdra was already skinny, she got it in her head that she needed a tummy-tuck – she didn't though. But there's always a doctor who is willing to do anything as long as they can charge you for it and Nevdra found one. Of course, Nevdra is as good at following directions as you'd expect her to be. And that even goes for aftercare instructions. So, when Nevdra thought that she was fully healed, she did her own thing instead of following the directions as given. And that caused a severe infection that resulted in necrosis and months of recovery time. Sadly, Nevdra had no one to take care of her – as incredible as it is, no one in her family helped her recover. I know this because I talked to her often and asked her if she needed anything or if there was anything that I could do to help. Nevdra always declined though, but I think that I was one of the few people that actually talked to her during that time. I did feel bad for Nevdra since I had a spare room at my house, but I knew that my wife at the time wouldn't go for me offering it to Nevdra and helping her out even though nothing had ever happened between Nevdra and me before that.

After that in 2020, Nevdra promised to help me put up campaign signs before Election Day[10]. But when it came time to meet up for me to give her the signs, she ghosted me. Afterwards, Nevdra told me that she couldn't because her aunt had passed away so she was with her family. That was very unfortunate, but completely understandable. And then Covid hit the U.S.

Sushi with Satan

Towards the end of August 2022, I was craving sushi and I mentioned it to Nevdra so we ended up agreeing to grab some for lunch.

---

[10] I ran for family court judge and this was for the primary race.

We agreed to meet at 11:00 AM – I generally like to take my lunch early. Turns out that the place that we were going to meet up at didn't open until 11:30 AM so we ended up going somewhere else. It was interesting as I really was just meeting up with Nevdra as old friends catching up. Nevdra even wore workout clothes, so didn't think much of it. But, Nevdra did the nervous nonstop talking thing during the entire lunch. I thought it was cute, but didn't think much of it. Nevdra called me while I was on the way back to the office to just keep talking and to apologize for talking so much during the lunch. Again, I thought it was cute and kind of flattering. We did agree to meet up again for lunch at some point so that we could go to the one place that we had originally planned on.

But because of our schedules and her getting sick for like a week, it took about a month for us to meet up again. This time Nevdra wore a really tight black dress that showed off her figure. Now during the first lunch, I had mentioned that I was an immigration lawyer and Nevdra had told me that she wanted to get her citizenship. She also told me a story about how she looked into the citizenship process because she was going to marry an Arab guy for "papers" but it fell through because his actual wife asked for a picture of Nevdra and when he sent it to her, she basically said "Hell No!" Anyways, during the lunch this time Nevdra brought it up again implying that I should help her. Originally, I thought that I would just send Nevdra the paperwork for her to fill out on her own. But, Nevdra's ability to manage it on her own seemed "questionable" so then I thought that I probably should help her fill it out.

Now around this point, my wife at the time had already told me that she wanted a divorce. She had been saying that she wanted a divorce for years, but we would just keep going as if she hadn't asked. While we may have legally still been married, our marriage ended a long time ago. For instance, we hadn't been intimate for *at least* 6 months at that point. And it got to the point where at the end of our conversations on the phone I would tell her "I love you" and she would just say "bye" and when I would try to kiss her when she arrived home, she would move her head away. But, in all honesty, I was just going through the motions – the love between us had died and I was just being delusional and didn't want to accept it because I thought that we could just stay married for the sake of our daughters. But that wasn't true.

In fact, she had a laundry list of reasons why she wanted to divorce me. And when she told me her reasons, she wasn't upset or angry or emotional in any way. As a matter of fact, she said them with such a lack of emotion that she could have been giving me the weather. I had actively been trying to be a better husband and it didn't matter to her at all. That's when it hit me that she was serious and things really were over. Have you ever been called repulsive by someone who was supposed to be your significant other? Yeah, that hurts more than you would think that it would. During one of those conversations, I asked her "then why are you always so jealous" and she replied with "if you haven't noticed, I haven't been jealous in a long time; as a matter of fact, I wish that you would find someone else because that's the only way to get rid of a nigga[11]." Well, the full details of that story are for another time, but the important things to remember is that my ex-wife ended the relationship before I did anything with Nevdra and that I was coming from a relationship with absolutely no passion, affection, intimacy, love, or even respect.

At this point, I was starting to like Nevdra. I wasn't sure if she liked me since we had always been friends and never really hung out before. But the last two times that we did see each other, I did get the impression that Nevdra was attracted and interested me. So, the third time that we met, Nevdra came to my part of town and we met up at a restaurant there. Nevdra got lost on the way, but did make it. We took a little longer

---

[11] Before you get the wrong idea, my ex-wife is Black and didn't mean it in a racist way.

than we thought and Nevdra ended up canceling / rescheduling one of her appointments to spend more time with me. And at the end, I went to kiss her while she was sitting in her car. Nevdra was wearing a baseball cap, and I was so out-of-practice in that area that I ended up hitting my eye with the rim of her hat. But I did kiss her. Nevdra called me while she was on the road after she left saying "me gusto mucho ese beso"[12]. I mentioned hitting my eye on the rim of her baseball hat and she promised not to wear it again. Out of nowhere that same evening, Nevdra unexpectedly sent me a video of herself tanning nude. Mind you, we had not had any sexual or even romantic discussions at that point – we just kissed for the first time, just once and not in a making out way, earlier that day.

As you can probably guess, the next time we met up for lunch, we did more than just eat food. It was a little sweet as we made out outside of the restaurant like two high schoolers for like 20 minutes until we decided to go somewhere else.

Since I was still living at the house, but in a separate room (I had already agreed to give my wife at the time the divorce that she had been asking for years for and she had agreed that I could stay at the house until

---

[12] Translation: "I really liked that kiss"

after the holidays [it was October] so that we could give the girls at least one last Christmas as a family), Nevdra and me talked on the phone every night.

At one point, I looked up Nevdra's ex-husband's unsuccessful divorce public filing to try to grab his information and saw the name of her son as something completely different than what Nevdra told me what her son's name was. So, I was a little confused and asked Nevdra about it. She became upset that I was "investigating her" and she told me about her other son for the first time. I wasn't investigating Nevdra *per se*, but I am an attorney working on her case so of course I would do research AND it was a public record anyways. But after telling me how much she doesn't like people investigating her life and me explaining that any attorney worth their salt would have found that and the reason why I went looking for it, Nevdra calmed down enough to ask me what was going on between us because she was falling in love with me and wanted to be with me — not because she needed me because she doesn't need me[13], but because she just wanted to be with me. I told her that I was also falling in love with her as well.

---

[13] Yeah, I know, it was kind of weird that she would say that, but maybe she thought that it was a concern of mine given her past.

This was all before Nevdra's scheduled trip to Europe. We met up several times before she left and she got me to open up accounts on WhatsApp, TikTok, Instagram, and Snap Chat (I only had Facebook at the time) so that we could communicate while she was overseas. When she was in Europe, we did talk every day (sometimes multiple times) despite the time difference. During all of this, my ex-wife noticed that I seemed happy again and more like my old self. Ironically, before all of this, my ex-wife had actually said that "you're never going to find anyone and will spend every holiday alone." I guess that I proved her wrong and that must have hit her hard in the ol' pride. Long story short, she told me that I had to leave much sooner than January. We were still in October, so that was a big difference in time. I did find an apartment where I could move to on November 1st. Since I had the apartment and was going to pay the rent and utilities anyways and Nevdra and I agreed that we never wanted to be apart again, I asked Nevdra if she just wanted to move in with me and she said that she did. The apartment I chose was in the same suburb less than 10 minutes from the house since I wanted to stay close to my daughters. Originally, Nevdra didn't have a problem with this or my arrangement to pick my daughters up from school, keep them for an hour or so, and then drop them off at their mom's house. But that changed shortly after she moved in....

Boardwalk Nevpire

Nevdra did start moving in around November 1st, 2022. This is when the "love bombing" was in full effect. I went from a relationship with no passion to one that was all passion. Nevdra hung from my every word, wanted me to explain everything that I talked about to her, found me fascinating, laughed at all of my jokes, wanted to hear all of my stories, was very affectionate, and just made me feel like the most loved man in the world. She would tell me all of her dreams, her plans for the future, and wanted me to know everything about her past – the good, the bad, and the ugly so that I would know everything about her and no one could break us up by telling me something about Nevdra that I didn't know. And aside from the emotional intimacy, there was plenty of physical intimacy – we were making love every day and usually it was at least twice a day. So, I went from no sex for over 6 months, to sex twice a day up to five times in one day. One thing that is probably impolite to mention is that female narcissists kind of weaponize sex and use it to control men. We had so much sex, that I even started to rapidly lose weight from all of the exercise. My coworkers would see me and ask me how I lost so much weight. I would kind of just smile and say that I was eating healthier – which was also true as well.

But my one true weakness was and still is my daughters. And Nevdra knew that's what would really capture me. Like on November 10, 2022 when she said that "ya quiero conocerlas y que sean parte de mi vida"[14]. Before that, I kept sending Nevdra photos and videos of the girls just being their charming selves. The apartment was a two bedroom and two bathrooms unit. Since Nevdra liked taking a bath and the bathroom in the master bedroom only had a shower stall, she took over the guest bathroom. When the girls went to the apartment for the first time, Nevdra wasn't there so I took a video of them seeing the bathroom for the first time telling them that a very special friend wanted to make it pretty for them.

My dad was visiting from Panama, so he was staying[15] with us in the guest room while he was in town. The night before he arrived, Nevdra was so nervous that she threw up. But, when they met each other, they got along so well it was like watching two old friends. Nevdra had visited

---

[14] Translation: "I want to meet them and for them to be a part of my life."

[15] When I told my dad that I had left the house, the first thing that he said was "Wait, where am I going to be staying when I go visit?!"

Puerto Rico a few years prior, so they mostly talked about Puerto Rico. At that time, I also started talking to a cousin from my mom's side that happened to live in a neighboring town. There already aren't that many Panamanians in town, so having one of my mom's cousins living nearby was almost miraculous. I had never met this distant cousin, so we had decided to meet up while my dad was visiting. So, I had my dad in town (my daughters have spent a lot of time with their grandparents), meeting a new family member, and my homegirl invited the girls to her twins' birthday party – all on the same day. I figured that there wasn't going to be a better opportunity anytime soon for my daughters to meet Nevdra for the first time since it wouldn't be the only event that day.

On November 12, 2022, I went to pick up the girls with my dad and took them to a park while Nevdra got ready and then we went back to the apartment where Nevdra finally met the girls. I basically told them that she was the very special friend that decorated the bathroom and the apartment. At some point, we had to tell the girls what to call her. We were in the car when Nevdra pulled out her credit card which happened to have a Disney's "Frozen" design on it. Thinking quickly, I threw out "Elsa" like one of the main characters from that movie. Nevdra nodded in approval. And while the girls were a little skeptical that it was her real name at first, they ended up accepting it. So, from that moment on, the girls knew her as "Elsa". They were 3 and 5 at the time, so it stuck with them.

We met up with my cousin who brought her teenage children as well at a Mexican restaurant halfway between where we both lived. The stress of meeting my daughters had made Nevdra sick to her stomach most of the day prior to meeting them, but she ended up feeling well enough to eat by the time it came time to eat at the restaurant. Afterwards, it was time for the birthday party at a skating rink. We showed up after the party had started, but not too late. My three-year-old is a little shy, so she didn't interact with Nevdra too much. She did stay with Nevdra for a little bit and went with her to the bathroom. My oldest daughter, however, was a different story. She wanted to skate! Unfortunately, she actually didn't know how to. This was where Nevdra completely won me over. She essentially went on the skating rink floor and taught my daughter how to skate. Nevdra and her had an amazing time together with both of them smiling from ear-to-ear. It was such a long, eventful day, that the youngest even passed out on the way home.

Was it too soon to introduce the girls to Nevdra? Probably; but it seemed like too perfect of an opportunity to pass up. Whether it was too soon or not, it was done and there was no turning back. Afterall, at this point I was convinced that this was the woman that I was going to spend the rest of my life with so they had to meet each other sooner or later.

Obviously, the girls' mother did not agree with the timing… when she found out (presumably from our daughters), she was pissed. Now she didn't tell me anything, but she made it very clear. *See*, she went ahead and found Nevdra's mugshot from her recent public intoxication arrest. I know what you're thinking, but that one shouldn't have happened. Nevdra had gone to a Daddy Yankee concert with her friend and had drinks at the concert. Nevdra was not driving. Her friend got pulled over leaving the concert for drinking and driving while Nevdra was in the car. When he got arrested, they took Nevdra (who was sitting in the car) in for public intoxication. They didn't even give Nevdra the opportunity to find a ride home so she wouldn't have been drunk in public – which she wasn't up until the police officer made her.

Anyways, I'm pretty sure that my ex got Nevdra's name by going through my personal files when I still had my stuff at the house. I never did any legal work outside of my job back then, so it probably made her suspicious that I was helping Nevdra do her citizenship and she saw Nevdra's real name on the documents. In the middle of a conversation one time, she said Nevdra's name but it didn't register in my brain when she said it and I kept talking about whatever we were talking about. My ex didn't bring Nevdra up again because she probably thought that it wasn't Nevdra since (1) I didn't even react when she said Nevdra's name and (2) Nevdra was in Europe at the time, so she probably thought that there's no way that I could be talking to Nevdra.

But somehow, she figured it out and then found her mugshot. I had posted something randomly on Facebook unrelated to Nevdra, the birthday party, meeting my cousin, or even the girls, and my ex commented on my post with the mugshot. I immediately deleted it. But then she changed her banner picture to the mugshot and then commented on another one of my posts with the same mugshot again. So as much as I didn't want to block her[16], she didn't leave me much of a choice.

Unfortunately, Nevdra found out about it and she did not take it well. From what would become a trend, she responded to adversity / conflict by getting drunk. Nevdra got drunk at her old apartment after she had finished with a client. Even though she was almost 50 years old,

---

[16] I didn't want to block her because that would mean that I wouldn't have access to the pictures and videos of our daughters that were on her Facebook page.

Nevdra never learned how to deal with conflicts and instead just avoids them with alcohol.

My dad was still staying at the apartment, so I was trying to keep him from finding out what was going on. I went to try to talk to Nevdra at her old apartment. It did not go well...

Nevdra streamed some music videos while we were laying on her couch. But at one point Nevdra just flipped out and started throwing stuff at me. She threw a bottle at me that broke on the floor. Nevdra also threw some hookah stuff at me that broke as well. She even tried to hit me with the hookah hose like she was Indiana Jones or the Ghost Rider. I was dealing with it (Nevdra missed because I dodged) up until she pulled a knife on me; that's when I decided to leave. Apparently, Nevdra actually ran out after me because she didn't want me to go. But I had already gotten in the car and left. I was halfway home when Nevdra found her phone and called me. I believe that her daughter Jackie was trying to prevent Nevdra from calling me, but Nevdra managed to call me anyways. Nevdra begged me to come back for her because she wanted to come home to our apartment. So you guessed it, I turned around and went and picked her up.

It was late at night / early in the morning when we finally made it back. My dad – thankfully – was already asleep. Nevdra also begged me not to tell my father about what happened. My dad did comment "regresaron tarde anoche"[17] to which I just replied with a "yeah…" and left to work. The excuse that I gave myself for Nevdra's behavior was that she was reacting to what my ex-wife did and couldn't deal with the helplessness that she felt…

Sunday Not So Funday

So the first "incident" happened after Nevdra met my father and my daughters, right? Right?! No… unfortunately, the very first incident happened on Sunday, November 6, 2022 which was almost immediately after Nevdra moved in and before she met anyone.

Between moving in and getting used to living together, we hadn't really gone anywhere together. So, Nevdra said that we should do the whole "Sunday Funday" thing since her DJ friend was playing at a club with a big outside area. I hadn't really gone out in years, so it sounded fun and I was excited to go. Nevdra said that we'll just check it out for a few hours since I have to work in the morning.

The night started out decent enough with smoking some hookah while having some drinks, dancing, and listening to music. By the end of

---

[17] Translation: "ya'll got in late night"

the night, Nevdra was drunk and was telling people that she didn't want to go home with me. Not sure where that came from because I thought that we were having a good time and I didn't do anything to make her feel that way. It was pretty awkward because during the night, her DJ friend hung out with us off and on when he wasn't talking to other people. He didn't really want to get involved, but at the same time he kind of let security know that I was cool and that Nevdra was just really drunk so not to pay any mind to her. Even the bouncers had that "yeah, we don't really know what to do, so you're on your own bro and it's closing time so figure it out somewhere else" vibe to them.

So, on one hand I can't force her to come with me to our apartment and on the other hand I can't just leave her there on her own (I mean I could have, but I'm a gentleman so it wasn't an option for me plus this is the woman that I love). Well, Nevdra leaves with me and I'm kind of letting her walk in front of me as we walk towards my car – talking crazy the whole time. We make it to the car and drive off. About halfway there Nevdra starts saying that she wants to go to her apartment but she doesn't have her keys on her so even if I wanted to leave her there, we had to go to our apartment to grab her keys first anyways. Nevdra opens the car door and prevents me from closing it by using her foot to keep it open while I'm driving. She was wearing heels – not sure why that's important, but I always remember that detail for some reason. Since we're on the highway at o' drunk thirty and would be pretty noticeable by any police officer, I get off at the next exit which was only one exit early coincidentally. Maybe there was something about that exit because I've had to get off on that exit when there were other incidents a few times. At least that exit has a smooth exit ramp. While on the feeder, Nevdra grabs the wheel and tries to make us crash – good thing that we weren't on the highway anymore. Thankfully, I'm able to maintain enough control of the wheel so that we don't crash. Somehow, we make it home. I left Nevdra in the room and I think that I slept on the couch for a couple of hours before going to work. I do remember that Nevdra was asleep when I left for work in the morning.

Nevdra texted me shortly before lunch saying that we need to talk. I told her that I can come home for lunch to talk in person. When I get home, she's still in bed and tells me that she'd hate for something so beautiful like what we have between us to end for something that she did. Nevada explained that she has a demon inside of her that comes out when she drinks too much and she hates it, but can't control it. She asks for me to forgive her. Not knowing any better, I told her that I considered it an outlier, something that was so far from what I've had with her, that I consider it as something a stranger did that won't happen again so there's no reason to dwell on it. And I forgive her and we made love a few times and eventually eat lunch / dinner. I didn't return to work that day.

Back to the Love Bombing Phase

After my dad left back to Panama, it was around my birthday[18]. Nevdra had made dinner reservations for that Saturday, but we had my daughters on that Friday as well. She actually suggested taking them to a City Center place so that they can celebrate my birthday. Even though it was a little cold, there was an open park area where my daughters ran around and played for a while until we went to get dinner. We walked to a sushi place near there where the girls had some chicken fried rice that we ordered, but they really enjoyed themselves playing with the chopsticks. Nevdra tried teaching my 5-year-old daughter (who turned 6 the following weekend) how to use them and she did actually learn how to. Afterwards we went for ice cream there. There was one thing that was pretty adorable and it was that every time Nevdra tried to get me to take a video of her doing her trademark "walk", my daughters would run up and try to hug her or be around her no matter how far away they were when she started the recording. Nevdra did manage to do it once before the girls got in the video

---

[18] Scorpio baby!

in case you were wondering. I wouldn't even be surprised if Nevdra still has it on her social media.

The next day was my actual birthday and Nevdra wanted to go all out on my birthday celebration. She made reservations at a fancy place in town. Originally, Nevdra had told her friend about it and her friend had invited herself to the dinner. Fortunately, her friend bailed before that night, so it was just us two. Although, believe it or not, that would have probably been the only time that I would have met one of her female friends as she NEVER introduced me to any of her female friends during the entire relationship. I know, it's a red flag – one of several that I saw but chose to ignore.

But, back to the actual birthday celebration. Even though it wasn't a milestone birthday, Nevdra made it feel like one. She bought this beautiful cake that was baked in the shape of law books with a gavel (I'm an attorney). Nevdra sang happy birthday to me at the restaurant, toasted to me, fed me good food, and just made me feel loved. Definitely among the top two birthday celebrations that I've had in my four decades on this Earth. Now, Nevdra did get slightly upset that I didn't offer to buy her another drink during the dinner. I've never been a real big drinker, so one drink to toast with seemed perfect and it never crossed my mind to drink anything more than that. And even if I did, generally when a person invites someone to dinner, the invitee usually doesn't pay for anything during the dinner. But after we got up from the table and she mentioned it, I bought her a drink at the bar before we left. Nevdra probably wanted to keep drinking but she didn't push the issue when I was ready to end the night on a high note. But other than that, it was an amazing night.

Thanksgiving 2022

I always thought that there were some things that you can never say without meaning it because you can't take it back. One of those things is that "I don't love you". So, no matter how mad I ever got with anyone, I would never say those words unless I truly meant it. The first time that Nevdra said that to me, I didn't see her being drunk making any difference to the veracity of it. So, I was crushed because I thought that she didn't love me. The next day Nevdra asked me why I was so distraught. I told her that it's because she doesn't love me any more, doesn't want to be with me any more, and let me know very clearly the night before. Nevdra's counter was that maybe at that small moment she could have meant it, but that her saying that she doesn't love me one time shouldn't count more than all of the other times that she tells me that she loves me because she does love me and does want me in her life. I guess that Nevdra could tell that I wasn't exactly feeling her explanation because she posted a short video on her social media that she made of herself spinning around in a green dress where the audio starts off with "para que te quede claro[19]..." and it then starts playing a song saying how much she wants to be with me.

November is also the month of Thanksgiving. Even though we had realistically been together less than a month, we did live together more or less. So, Nevdra decided to take me to her family's Thanksgiving party. By then I had already re-met her daughter Jackie – I had met her once before at one of Nevdra's birthday parties where I was talking to Nevdra and Jackie comes up to say something to her mom and Nevdra was like "Oh this is my daughter Jackie", I was like "oh cool, nice to meet you", and that was basically the whole interaction. Although Jackie lived with Nevdra when we started dating, I wanted to "meet" her in a more formal manner since I was dating her mother and stealing her roommate away. But one of the times that I went to help Nevdra move some stuff from the apartment, I crossed paths with Jackie on the stairs. That meeting was just as anticlimactic as you're thinking it was.

---

[19] Translation: "so that it's clear to you"

So, I had met Jackie already, but hadn't met the rest of her family. Well, when her brother Hummer saw me, he said that he remembers me. It is very possible since we were both at one of Nevdra's birthday party or maybe two but I just didn't think that I was memorable enough to remember. He works in clubs, so he meets a lot of people and I usually don't stand out unless I have an actual conversation with that person. I knew that at least one of Nevdra's brothers (she has two), her sister Claudia, her mother, a bunch of nephews / nieces and cousins, and – her son, Roger, would be there. From the terrible stories about her mother growing up that Nevdra told me, I didn't care much about meeting her mother; but her son (the only one she acknowledges and still has a relationship with) was a different story. I was most nervous about meeting him – and it wasn't because she told me that he's been in and out of prison and has a history of getting into physical fights essentially beating up every boyfriend that she's ever had.

It wasn't a bad party to be honest. The food was delicious and everyone was cool; basically, a typical Hispanic Thanksgiving. One weird thing that happened was that when I asked Hummer where the bathroom was, he not only walked me to it, but went in with me. He started telling me a story about how he used to be a pimp – but a *nice* pimp that never hurt any of his "charges" – and that while he did time for being a pimp, the girls actually testified on his behalf, minimizing his sentence. He also offered me cocaine, which I politely declined. Not that I have anything against drugs *per se*, it's just never been my thing. I think that he was testing me as he started telling me that it doesn't matter how cool he is with someone, he won't let them drink and drive even if he has to punch the dude out and take his keys until he sobers up. Guess, it's only guys that he cares about them drinking and driving because his sister Nevdra does it religiously even without NEVER having had a driver's license. Since I know my limits and stop drinking before I get anywhere near the point where I can't drive, it didn't phase me. That and he seemed to really respect the fact that I had served in the Army. Well, it's a good thing that I don't have performance anxiety because I was able to pee and leave the bathroom without incident. Yeah, it was weird, but when we got drug tested in the Army, there was always at least one dude watching you pee into the cup. My thought on it was always "fuck it, enjoy the view!"

Anyways, mom was cool. She was super nice to me and made sure that I tried all of that good Salvadorean food – Nevdra served me the first plate, but her mom kept giving me more food after that. Claudia and Jackie were cool. The other family members were at least 10 years younger than me, so there wasn't much interaction, but they were cool.

As for Roger – things started off great. We had some pretty good getting to know each other interactions and even exchanged phone numbers. I didn't notice that he was drinking alcohol and that it was affecting him – guess that's an ongoing theme with me. Apparently, he's a pot head and generally doesn't drink and can't handle his alcohol. At one point, he texts me while sitting across the table from me that he wants to talk to me "man to man". Again, I didn't see anything wrong with this and *I'm a man* and figured if he wants to "man up" and talk to me about something, it's no problem. This transitions into a "come talk to me outside" situation so I go with him outside. Not a "come fight me outside" kind of thing, but a "let's just talk outside one on one without everyone around and where we can hear each other" thing. At least that's what I thought. Maybe he meant it as the "come fight me outside" situation, but it never crossed my mind since I hadn't done anything to him and I thought that we were just getting to know each other.

So we step outside and I suggest that we chill by / on top of my car. He starts talking about how he loves his mom and if I hurt his mom, then he'll hurt me. Didn't phase me since I was in love with Nevdra and I couldn't even envision a scenario where I'd ever hurt her. So, I was like "cool, we're on the same page" and I can respect him for looking out for his mom. In hindsight, I realized that he was looking for excuses to "swing on me" but I never gave him any. I think that it ended up being one of those "ugh, I want to hate this dude, but I can't because he's actually pretty cool" situations. After a few minutes I see Hummer and Jackie stick their heads out the door. Guess they figured that we'd be fighting by then. Nevdra kept coming out to tell me to come back into the house. But he said that he wanted to talk *man to man*, so I felt like I couldn't disrespect him by not treating him like a man. I really wasn't worried about him fighting me. I've dealt with my fair share of knuckleheads, so deescalating a violent person came second-nature to me. Only one time during our conversation did he start getting a little riled up, but it wasn't actually directed towards me so I was able to calm him down fairly easily.

At some point, the conversation had run its course so we returned inside. He was emotional so Nevdra comforted him and then he went to sleep in one of the rooms. Afterwards, Nevdra told me that she thought that he may have some sort of Oedipus Syndrome and possibly be a closeted gay man. After getting to know him later on, I don't believe either is true. I think that Roger just has a lot of anger inside of him from feeling abandoned by Nevdra and his father growing up and his mother's paramours were an easy target for that rage. Sadly, I think that I was the only regular, decent, somewhat normal male figure that he's ever had in his life.

All of this pretty much ended the party for Nevdra. She was upset with me that I went outside to talk to Roger against her wishes and really thought that he was going to fight me which meant that she would have to take his side if we were to fight. Nevdra was like "it's time to get the Hell out of here." I wanted to be my normal respectful self and properly say goodbye to everyone and thank the host for a good time. Nevdra's mom offered to fix me a to-go plate which my fat ass happily accepted the offer. However, Nevdra was basically like "Fuck no, you're not getting a to-go plate, the fuck's wrong with you!" I was very disappointed because the food was good. It was something that we laughed about when he looked back at it...

A few days after that Thanksgiving, it was my oldest daughter's sixth birthday. We got my two daughters the night before and spent the day with them. Nevdra actually looked happy spending time with them in the pictures that we took. She even fell asleep with my daughters laying next to her. If you ask me why I stayed as long as I did in what became an ever increasingly toxic relationship, it would be because I was holding on to moments like this and was hoping that life would be more like *that* than the bad stuff.

Café Cubano

Nevdra used to like smoking hookah when we first started seeing each other. I smoked it for the first – and one of the few times in my life – with her one time before we moved in together. Maybe she was a little embarrassed about breaking her own hookah pipe setup when she tried to hit me with it that one time at her apartment, but on one night, Nevdra wanted to go out together to have a night out. At this point, I've already gotten a little skeptical about going out in public with Nevdra to go drinking so she even offered to pay for everything. I reluctantly agreed and even left my wallet at home to not tempt myself to reject Nevdra's offer to pay. Actually, Nevdra wanted to go to the same hookah bar where I went with her to smoke my first hookah.

The first time that we went, we mostly just hung out outside smoking hookah while talking about her friends that I also knew – since she was my best friend's friend, most of the people that we mutually knew were people that I also met through Cindy. But this time, we stayed inside the club area more than the outside area. We did smoke some hookah outside, but for the most part we were dancing and listening to music inside… and drinking of course. At one point, Nevdra saw a group of Jackie's friends but she said that she didn't care since Jackie and her family had already met me anyways.

Towards the end of the night, it was time to close out the tab. The tab wasn't too bad as we had only purchased a couple of hookahs and the drinks weren't terribly expensive. And this is where things take their usual turn… the waitress comes back with Nevdra's credit card saying that it didn't go through. Nevdra checks her account online and assures the waitress that the card should be working so to keep trying it because something must be wrong on their end. Yes, Nevdra was already drunk at this point. This causes it to get locked because they tried to run it one too many times. I went inside with Nevdra's credit card after she unlocked it to give it to the club so that they could run it. When I get back, I'm accused of conspiring with the waitress to steal Nevdra's money. Lovely!

At this point the club is closed and Nevdra's credit card never went through. Since we were the only open account still left, they couldn't leave until we settled up. Again, I didn't have my wallet with me. The security guard and the waitress keep trying to explain to Nevdra that her card isn't going through and Nevdra keeps insisting that there's nothing wrong with her card. Since Nevdra is Nevdra she starts insulting Cubans because the waitress is Cuban and everyone that we've seen that works there is also Cuban and Cubans love going there. The security basically says "hold up, I'm Cuban and you're insulting me because I'm not a thief like you're saying all Cubans are". The solution ends up being the waitress pays the tab to close it out and I Zelle her the money to cover it. No one really liked that solution, but no one had a better option. Luckily, Nevdra was too drunk to realize that it meant that the waitress had to give me her personal phone number and me verifying her name for that to happen. Guess that it was obvious that Nevdra wouldn't like this, so we kind of did that out of her presence. When everything was confirmed, we were more or less escorted out of the club while Nevdra was still insulting all of Cuba and everyone of Cuban descent.

First Domestic Violence Case

On Saturday, December 17, 2022, Nevdra and I basically spent all day watching romantic movies. During the time that I was with Nevdra, she had a mobile business doing body contouring — mostly using a machine with multiple heads that could do treatments using radiofrequency, ultrasonic cavitation, vacuum, electric muscle stimulation, etc. Didn't know it at the time, but most of her clients were just her old friends who probably also had drinking problems. Nevdra would drive to their places with her machine; each treatment being an hour or two depending on how many body areas that they had done that session. When we first started seeing each other, Nevdra might do up to two or three on the same day. If you remember when we first started hanging out, Nevdra actually cancelled an appointment so that she could spend more time with me. I remember thinking "wow, she must really like me if she's going to give up money just so that she wouldn't have to leave".

Back to that day, Nevdra had a client that evening. It was a Saturday, so figured that I'd just chill at home until she came back in a couple of hours. Since I assumed that Nevdra would just do her work and come back, when Nevdra texted me that she was done but was going to stop by her old apartment that she shared with her daughter, I didn't think much of it. I was still in a romantic type of mood from watching all of those movies earlier, so I told her to say "hello to my future stepdaughter." Pretty sure that Nevdra already had at least some drinks in her because she took that the *wrong* way. First, she thought that I was telling her to say "hello" to her client. When I cleared that up, Nevdra didn't take it any better. I tried to explain that I was trying to be "cute" letting her know that I was thinking about my future with her after watching all of those movies together. Nope! Nevdra responded with the accusation that I had something with her daughter Jackie. I, of course, denied it and let her know how wrong that would be. But Nevdra clearly was convinced otherwise, because when she got home, she basically started attacking me.

Not only did Nevdra start throwing things, but she started attacking my face, neck, and chest with her hands. At one point, Nevdra pushed this giant bluish glass jar onto the floor. Surprisingly, it didn't break but it hit the floor with a giant thud. I think that's what caused the neighbor to call the police that night. The police report actually quotes the neighbor as saying "it sounds like they're killing each other." Well, it wasn't "each other" because I was just trying to calm Nevdra down and when that wasn't working, I tried to get out of there. I remember trying to put on my shoes and jacket when Nevdra flipped me over the back of the couch with a bar stool across my neck trying to choke me with it. I think that's when I lost my cell phone because I found it in the couch cushions after I came back to the apartment later on; it must have slid out of my pocket when she flipped me over.

I managed to get out of the apartment somehow and went downstairs (we lived on the second floor). I was barely down the stairs trying to figure out what happened and what to do now when I saw like six police officers with flashlights across the common area on the other side of the building. Figured that if I ran, I would look really suspicious. So I just kept walking casually in the same direction that I was going.

It didn't take long for them to spot me. They asked what apartment I lived in and when I told them, one of them said "Oh, so you know why we're here." I responded with "I can take a guess." Two of them stayed with me, while the rest went off – to the apartment to speak with Nevdra, I imagine. I handed one of them my wallet while the other one patted me down. One of the officers tells the other officer, basically "look man, he's bleeding." I was surprised by that since I didn't know that I was bleeding. But sure enough, I had cuts and scratches all over my face, neck, and chest area[20]. It's funny how fast their attitude towards me changed at that point.

They asked me what happened, so I basically told them that Nevdra came home angry because she took what I said as me having something going on with her daughter. They asked me if Nevdra did that to me, so I told them that "I'm not going to lie, so yeah, she did." I did say that she didn't choke me because I knew that it would escalate things against her if I did. But I let them know that I was her attorney for her immigration stuff,

---

[20] They had me lift up my shirt, so that's how they saw those.

so I would prefer it if they didn't do anything to her when they asked me if I wanted her arrested. When they asked what I wanted to do then, I really didn't have an answer. I think that I just said that I just wanted Nevdra to just have some time to cool off. The officers kept me downstairs and kept talking to me but we did move a little closer to the stairwell. I kept telling them that I didn't want to press any charges and didn't want Nevdra arrested. I also declined a protective order and to make a written statement. They clearly weren't waiting for me to give them my consent, because when they walked me up the stairs, I saw the officers taking Nevdra away in handcuffs going down the stairwell on the other side.

One of the officers had a camera and told me that he needed to take pictures of me. He took pictures of my face, my neck, my chest, and my hands. This was right outside of the apartment. One of the arresting officers came back and asked me if I knew where Nevdra's cell phone was because she was asking for it. I entered the apartment for the first time accordingly. There was broken glass everywhere. Apparently, Nevdra threw more glasses or maybe pushed her cocktail cart really hard and glasses flew off after I left. One of the officers even warned me to watch my step because of the glass on the floor when I opened the door. I found Nevdra's phone on the floor under the couch, I believe, and gave it to the officer. After that, they gave me the victims' rights information along with the card with the incident information and left. It was just me and the broken glass at that point.

I really didn't know what to do besides just clean up the broken glass...

After a while, I get a call from the jail from my assaulter, Nevdra. I accept and Nevdra asks me for my help in getting her out and gives me her sister's and her brother's phone numbers so that I can let them know what's going on. I know what you're thinking, and no, Nevada didn't give me her daughter's phone number. The timing on the call was interesting because it cut off right after she asked me if I still love her and before I could respond. Since it was so late,[21] I texted Nevdra's brother and sister letting them know that she's been arrested and I'll give them more details when they finish processing her. I called the jail where Nevdra was at, and they confirmed that she was there. I asked if I could do an attorney visit, and they said that it would be fine but that they'll probably move her in a few hours.

---

[21] At 01:47 AM, I texted "Sorry for the late text; this is [Nevdra]'s boyfriend, Robert. She wanted me to let you know that she's at the [...] jail. She's being transferred to [...] County in the morning"

As I was getting ready to drive to the jail, the officer calls me back to let me know that I won't be able to see Nevdra after-all. Unfortunately, I didn't get notice of the call or the voicemail until I got to the jail. The jail was about 2 blocks away, so it wasn't a terrible drive or anything. But when I get there, the officer on duty informs me that when he saw that my name was the same as the victim, he talked to his supervisor and the supervisor told him that I can't visit with her even if I am her attorney. Probably doesn't come up much – and maybe it was the first time that situation happened – but understandable. He told me that she'll be transferred in the morning to the county jail and that I should be able to visit with her there.

In the morning, I finally get a call from Nevdra's sister that starts with "I don't have any money for bail". I didn't ask and Nevdra didn't even have any bail set at that time anyways. Nevdra called me later that morning when she had been transferred to the county and I updated her sister. And her brother? He never responded to the text. Funny thing though is that he gave me his number another day, and when I went to save it, it turned out to be that same number.

I did get to go visit Nevdra that day while she was incarcerated. Because it was the weekend, the judge had gone home for the day before

Nevdra got there and wouldn't be back to arraign her until the next day meaning that Nevdra had to spend the night in the county jail. During the visit, Nevdra was very apologetic and remorseful. She even said that she wouldn't blame me if I called the police on her. So, if I had, there would have been no reason for me not to let her know at that moment. I would have to remind Nevdra of this multiple times after she would continue to accuse me of calling the police on her so that she could be arrested. Of course, her underlying criminal behavior didn't have *anything* to do with her getting arrested and charged – it was my "betrayal" of contacting the authorities that solely caused her troubles with the law. During the visit, Nevdra told me that even though she was freezing cold the whole time and only recently got a blanket, the worst part was not knowing if I still loved her because the phone call had cut off right when she asked me and before she could hear my response. As what would become a trend, Nevdra promised to stop drinking even saying that she'd go so far as going to an inpatient facility if needed.

After the visit, I had to wait for Nevdra to see a judge which she did early the next day. Afterwards, I went through the process of bailing her out. Unfortunately, in between starting the process and actually getting released, I had to pick up my daughters. So, I had to take my daughters with me to go meet with the bail bondsmen in the waiting area of the jail while they watched videos on my phone. Luckily, we were the only ones there. Since they were so young, I told them that we had to go pick up Nevdra from work because she didn't have her car.

I brought Nevdra a change of clothes and then we left the jail after she changed. In my rush to get Nevdra out as soon as possible, I neglected to get gas before getting to the jail. As such, the fuel indicator actually hit *zero more miles* as I pulled into the first gas station that we got to on the way back. Nevdra was starving, so she got something to eat at the gas station. Then we all went home.

Nevtide 2022

It was basically the same week of Christmas that Nevdra was released from jail. Luckily, all of the gifts were already bought, wrapped, and under the Christmas tree before all of that craziness happened. During the week, Nevdra had to go meet up with the bail company, but that was about it. Christmas itself was pretty low key – lazy Christmas Eve with the girls opening gifts, watching movies, special breakfasts and dinners, taking pictures, etc. Christmas Day itself was just Nevdra and me after we dropped off the girls to their mom's.

Nevdra had an important medical appointment on December 29, 2022. Since I had to pick up the girls early that day, I thought that the best plan was to drop off Nevdra at her appointment about an hour early and then go pick up the girls and then return to pick up Nevdra from her appointment. The timing pretty much worked out as Nevdra was done about 15 minutes before we returned for her. Successful planning – cool, right? Not for Nevdra. She had an issue with the fact that she had to do the diagnostic appointment by herself.

If you think that New Year's Eve 2022 would have been a good time, then I'm sorry that you're so optimistic. It sucks to be that optimistic – trust me, I know. With everything that has already happened, we decided on a lowkey New Year's Eve with us having dinner with her daughter at our apartment – yes that daughter… It was actually Jackie's first time in our apartment, but there really wasn't any issue with her. I picked up dinner for us, we ate dinner together, and then Jackie left. Not surprisingly, we started drinking during dinner and we were all probably already drunk by the time that Jackie left for her night of partying.

After Jackie left, Nevdra did what she did best when she's drunk and started being belligerent. Her main issue this time was to accuse me of calling the police on her the night of her arrest and filing charges on her.

At one point Nevdra said that Jackie stood outside the apartment when I was out getting the food and Jackie said that she couldn't hear anything from outside the apartment; pretty sure that was a lie and that didn't happen at all, but it is some impressive gaslighting. It got so bad that I left the house before Nevdra got the chance to assault me again. Since I was drunk and didn't really have anywhere to go, I just hung out on the apartment complex grounds by the lake – luckily there were still fireworks going off to help pass the time. Of course, I was inexplicably accused of running off to my ex-wife's house to hook up with her. Yeah, that made no sense to me either…

The next day, on January 2nd, 2023, I went with Nevdra to help her daughter Jackie (yeah, I guess that her drunken accusations on December 18th were wild figments of her imagination) move from the apartment that they used to share to one across the street in a sister apartment complex. For some reason, I still felt bad about taking Jackie's roommate, making me feel some obligation to her. So helping Jackie move was my chance to meet my obligation to her. When I got there, it was basically Jackie, me, and two other guys. Jackie was still in the process of packing, so Nevdra helped her with that while the two guys and I moved some of the big stuff.

I ended up renting the moving van since Jackie somehow has no credit and I think had a problem with her Driver's License at that time as well. I had to put it on my credit card, but Jackie paid me cash for it, so that was fine. The rest of Jackie's moving crew finally arrived after we made a few trips already. There was Jackie's female friend, that girl's boyfriend, and her obligatory gay male friend and his boyfriend. When they arrived, the other two guys left around the same time. Likewise, Nevdra also left to go to the store to buy some stuff for our apartment. She was frustrated by Jackie's lack of preparation for the move and was tired from helping Jackie pack her stuff. Yup, that means that I was basically the only person that was there from the beginning of the move to the end of the move. When we were finally done moving all of Jackie's stuff, Jackie invited all of us to dinner. Since I'm the one that rented the moving van, I went to turn it in while they got to the restaurant first. Although I was dead tired, Nevdra insisted that we go to dinner as it would be the only way that Jackie would "compensate" us.

Really should have skipped the invitation… Nevdra picked me up and we went straight to the restaurant. They had already started ordering, but we got there really right at the perfect time. Even back then, I wasn't really a big drinker so getting there after the first round of drinks was fine by me. In hindsight, between the food and alcohol that they all ordered, it probably would have been cheaper for Jackie to hire professional movers.

Since I was actually working moving things, I hadn't had the chance to really meet the moving posse. And they hadn't had the chance to meet me either. During the conversation, it came out that I was an attorney. Well, the boyfriend of Jackie's friend (I think his name was Mario) did need an attorney for a case that he had. He was seated a couple of people away from me so Jackie's gay best friend was sitting immediately next to me, while Nevdra was seated directly across from me. The gay best friend offered to take my number and give it to the dude later. Seems reasonable since Nevdra was looking for my card, but couldn't seem to find it. Oh no, not to Nevdra!

As soon as we left the restaurant, she started accusing me of wanting something with the gay guy because I gave him my number to give to his close friend (the potential client). Nevdra thought that because the gay guy engages in prostitution at least occasionally, he was going to claim me as a customer. Mind you, I have never been attracted to other guys or had any same-sex experiences – unlike Nevdra who had already admitted a few to me before. As usual, I'm pretty sure that she was projecting onto me like always. Nevdra kind of made a little scene outside the restaurant so things got a little awkward with these people that I just met for the first time. Needless to say, no one ever called to hire me or reached out to me at all.

Even with an open domestic violence case, Nevdra didn't stop. On January 23, 2023, I sent Nevdra a picture of a cut she made on my left eyebrow with the rest of my face all red from being hit by her. She responded by sending me an uncaptioned picture of a large gash over her eye – it was an old picture from who knows when from before me because in the picture Nevdra had her nails done in a color that she's never had since we've been together. Understanding what Nevdra was trying to imply, I let her know that it was clearly an old picture because of the nail color and she never responded.

If I had to guess from when that picture was, I would go with it being from her time with her ex-boyfriend she refers to as "El Cubano". Not sure why she refers to him that way since she's dated another Cubano before, but this is the one with the initials "DC". He was the one that stole credit card numbers and made copies of them. If you ever had unauthorized charges on your account from that time frame, you'd be happy to know that Nevdra and him used them for such things as furniture, sneakers, fishing equipment, and cigarettes for him and alcohol for her.

Looking back at the stories that Nevdra told about him, I'm pretty sure that she would instigate and start the fights (probably hitting him first) and him not being a real man, would hit her back. But since he was bigger and stronger than her, he would cause more damage. Funny thing is that I don't think that she really liked him that much given how one time she asked if I could look him up to see why he wasn't getting bail saying "I have a friend whose family wants to know why he's still in jail." Never said "boyfriend" even though they were dating at the time and back then the only difference that it would have made to me was that I would have probably advised her to dump that loser after looking at his criminal record and the risk that she ran of being deported with all that. Matter of fact, she would even tell me that no one took her to her tummy tuck surgery and she went alone back when we were talking during her recovery. But when we had an argument, Nevdra let it slip that he did take her and then got arrested for credit card theft / fraud almost immediately during the start of her recovery – which would have been exactly at the same time that she asked me to look him up. So shady…

February Family Fun

On February 4, 2023, Nevdra's sister Claudia and her two children (daughter and son) came to visit our apartment. Of course, you know that alcohol was going to be involved. Apparently, a lot of people say that Nevdra's niece looks strikingly similar to Nevdra when she was younger. Guess that's why Nevdra seems to have a particular affinity for her. Even though she was 13 or 14 at the time, she still did her own makeup, eyebrows, and hair. Nevdra also offered her some of her old clothes that no longer fit her. Most of the clothes seemed a little too skimpy for a girl her age, but not enough to be vulgar or anything. While I didn't really talk to her this time, we did have a pretty good conversation another time a few months later when they came down to hang out at the pool at our apartment complex. She was pretty cool, and nothing like Nevdra was at her age. She was just a normal teenage girl that reminded me a little of my own niece. She had told me that Nevdra is like the black sheep of the family and that she doesn't believe that Nevdra deserves all of the criticism that she gets. I really, really hope that she can get away from all of that craziness of her family and that nothing of Nevdra rubs off on her. Her mom seems to have matured past whatever craziness of her youth and seems to want to actively avoid drama, so I have hope. Likewise, I hope that her younger brother that also came to visit doesn't let being in that family change him. During that first visit, we got to hang out a little bit (only other male at the apartment) and he reminded me of my son when he was that age. He was into anime and video games, so we really got along. He's also really good at drawing, especially manga style. By the way, if I haven't mentioned this before, I am a bit of a nerd.

At one point, they start to run out of alcohol because we don't really have alcohol at the house and Nevdra's sister seemingly underestimated how much they would drink with what she brought. I was asked to go get more alcohol since I was the only one who wasn't drinking. Nevdra was already pretty drunk by then. Asking me to leave – even if it was to buy more alcohol – was a blessing at that point and I leaped at the opportunity. Prior to this, things were getting a little uncomfortable since her sister kept telling her that she was on medicine and didn't really want to drink but Nevdra kept insisting that she keep drinking. Guess that Nevdra's sister only brought a limited amount of alcohol to try to control the situation, but alcohol, Nevdra, and control don't coexist together. Nevdra also took the opportunity to try to humiliate me in front of her sister (and niece I suppose who was listening to all this). Nevdra made two comments that stood out: "no lo soporto! No puede hace algo fácil[22]" and "Él va porque yo quiero las cervezas y él lo va hacer"[23].

---

[22] Translation: "I can't stand him! He can't do anything so easy"
[23] Translation: "He's going to go because I want beer and he will do it!"

Guess that figuring out what I was going to do in this situation was distracting to me because I ran over the curve with my car. And because it was already dark, it wasn't exactly the easiest thing to see if my car was damaged. But as a loving, caring girlfriend, Nevdra made sure that I was safe and that the car was okay as well. *Just kidding*, she completely ignored the fact that I ran over the curb and kept asking where I was with her beers and her credit card (oddly, Nevdra never had money for any bills, groceries, etc. but always seemed to have money for alcohol). After about an hour, her family left. Pretty sure that Nevdra probably further insulted me to her family before they left.

Nevdra tried to say that she wasn't drunk, but I reminded her of the things that she was saying of me in front of her family and how her drunkenness is always clear in her eyes – a look that I was already very, very familiar with at this point. Nevdra's response was that her family became uncomfortable because they had to wait too long for me to return with more alcohol because *that* makes a lot of sense. The same sister that texted me "I really hope you can help her out she really is not a bad person but the alcohol is bad… I know the cause of everything is the alcohol" after Nevdra's domestic violence arrest.

Oh, Nevdra did finally acknowledge the car incident after two hours by saying "tienes seguro"[24] and then accusing my ex-wife of letting the air out of my tires. *Obviously*, that's what caused me to run over the curb somehow. Oh, the same ex-wife that Nevdra had also accused me of going to see that night during the same time that we were texting back and forth because apparently, I'm *that* gifted to be having an argument over text while hooking up at the same time. Nevdra's concern for me only grew more loving as she locked the deadbolt on me when I tried to return home and I had to beg her to let me into the apartment to which I pay every single bill in. Nevdra had a problem with the lamp in the bedroom, and that's why she eventually let me back in – to figure out the problem...

Around this same time, Jackie got cosmetic surgery in the Dominican Republic because *of course she did*. Apparently, Jackie had a romance with a *tigre*[25] that she sees over there every now and then and she stayed with his family during her recovery. Not sure how much money Jackie paid those people, but they did take her to and from her appointments, cooked for her, and generally took care of her. But, regardless of how well or poorly they took care of her, Jackie still boarded

---

[24] Translation: "You have insurance"

[25] Dominican term for a "guy" usually in reference to a guy whom a woman claims as her own. Literally means "tiger"

a plane to return home a little earlier than recommended. As a result, Jackie had some complications.

By the way, I didn't know that they just straight up leave holes in your body for you to drain bloody fluid out of. Whoever came up with this whole liposuction surgery idea must have been a sadist or a cenobite or something. Anyways, Jackie got an infection and had to go to the hospital. When she got released, she actually came to our apartment to recover. We had a spare bedroom with its own bathroom that was really for my daughters, but they weren't spending the night with us at that time. Besides, Jackie likes pink juvenile girly stuff, so it was a great fit. The first couple of days were rather uneventful. My daughters came over and actually met Jackie for the first time. They introduced themselves and that was about it. They didn't say anything about it or had any real reaction otherwise.

One day Nevdra went to work, so it was up to me to take care of our convalescence guest. Jackie's boyfriend had bought a lot of healthy, recovery-assisting foods so I cooked some for her and basically left it for her in the room and picked up the used plates when she was done. No real interactions more than that.

It goes without saying that with the responsibility of caring for your sick daughter, Nevdra's priority was making sure that she could take the best possible care of her daughter. Just kidding! Nevdra got piss drunk one night and came home accusing my oldest daughter of talking shit about Jackie being in their room to me. Yes, my 6-year-old daughter! And in case you had that question – no, of course not; she barely cared let alone was bothered enough to say anything. Thankfully, the girls weren't there at this time.

So, instead of being the best mom that Nevdra could be to her recovering adult daughter, she got drunk enough to force her injured daughter to get up from her bedrest based on a drunken hallucination that not only made no sense, but had absolutely no basis in reality. Nevdra grabbed all of Jackie's stuff and ran off with her to Jackie's apartment where Nevdra remained with her for a couple of days. After Nevdra returned home, Nevdra would go drive to check on Jackie every day for about a week.

Being Nevdra's daughter, Jackie wouldn't let something like not being fully healed stop her from celebrating her birthday. So, on February 25, 2023, Jackie held her birthday party at the same place that Nevdra took me for my birthday. It's their go-to Brazilian steakhouse because Nevdra's brother Hummer is friends with the manager there and can occasionally get hook-ups or at least special treatment. Jackie rented out a private dining area for all of her guests – and there were a lot of us. It was decorated with balloons everywhere including balloons that spelled her name out. Since the last time that I saw Jackie was when Nevdra dragged her out of the apartment, it was kind of an awkward situation. But I sat close to Jackie's sugar daddy boyfriend who was paying for everything, so that helped since he's a cool dude who I actually consider a friend. Guess that having that trauma bond of what we went through with that family kind of helped with that as well.

But, a random girl in a skin tight green dress comes in with her man, walks behind me on the way to sit down, kisses me on the top of the head, and then proceeds to sit down in the open seats several seats down. I was so shocked that I froze up because I had no idea who this person is let alone why the fuck she would think that it was cool to kiss me on the top of the head. It was certainly not something that I would have ever imagined. As it turns out, it was Jackie's friend who helped her move with me. I didn't recognize her because that was the one and only time that I had ever seen her before and she was in sweats with no kind of glam and here she was dressed to kill.

Obviously, Nevdra took this as well as you'd expect with a couple of drinks in her already. Guess that my shock was not the "right" reaction for her. Nevdra said that I had the reaction of someone who had hooked up with a girl, but wanted to pretend like I don't know her. Things got to the point where I thought it was best for me to leave before Nevdra caused a huge scene – probably committing an assault against me in front of everyone – and ruined Jackie's birthday party. I discreetly told Jackie and her boyfriend that it was probably better for me to leave and if they could take care of Nevdra. I also took the opportunity to tell them that after actually spending time talking to me during the night, that if some of the things that Nevdra has said about me that I have said or done don't sound right because they don't seem to match my personality, then it's probably not true and I left it at that.

Well, I was hoping to give Nevdra some time to cool off and me being the idiot that I am, I felt bad about leaving her without a ride even though her whole family was basically there. What I hadn't anticipated was that they would keep buying Nevdra drinks and that her mom would start saying things like "if he didn't have anything to do with that woman, then he should come back and show everyone that you [Nedra] are his woman." Gee, I wonder where Nevdra gets it from?

So, Nevdra is texting me and calls me to tell me that. I really hadn't driven that far and was kind of hanging out close by just in case I had to come back to get Nevdra. I return about 15 minutes later which is also about 5 minutes before the restaurant closes. I try to tell Nevdra this, but she insists that I come upstairs. I park and go upstairs. Unfortunately for me, there was still time for me to buy her a drink – another thing that she insisted on when I got there. Of course, Nevdra hadn't let it go and ended up slapping me outside of the elevator in front of everyone (there's only one elevator that everyone takes since the restaurant is on the second or third floor). Since everyone has to leave through the same entrance / exit and the restaurant is closing, Jackie's friend is actually in the large crowd with us. I basically had to stop Nevdra from fighting her and that's how I "earned" my slap. The car ride home was what you'd expect. After getting physically stricken a few times, I tell Nevdra that she has assaulted me and that if she doesn't stop, I'm filing charges this time. Nevdra responds that there's no evidence, so I tell her that they can get my blood off of her rings that she was wearing. Nevdra wasn't completely devoid of reason because she immediately takes her rings off, rolls down her window, and throws them outside onto the freeway.

Springtime for Nevdra

Maybe it was the increasing temperature or maybe the pollen production or who knows why, but for some reason the drinking and violence seemed to ramp up. Jackie said that the "honeymoon period" of 3 months had ended already, so maybe that was it. But, in Spring I probably got the majority of my permanent scars by -quite literally – her hands. On March 22nd, 2023 Nevdra went full on cat demon and scratched up my chest, arm, and neck really bad. I remember that a few days afterwards Nevdra wanted to go to the pool with my daughters but I told her that I couldn't because I wouldn't be able to take off my shirt with all the bright new scratches on my chest and stomach especially. One of the few times that I saw regret in Nevdra's eyes was after I said that to her. But speaking of permanent marks on my torso, I guess that it's a good thing that I've been fat most of my life because some of the scratches were very near my stretch marks so after they healed up, they weren't as noticeable – well, to anyone other than me that is.

March 25, 2023 was a "memorable" one. On that day, Nevdra comes home drunk as usual. I'm in the living room where I stay not wanting to really deal with Nevdra while she goes into the bedroom talking her usual drunken abusive nonsense. Since the time that Nevdra goes into the bedroom from when she gets home, I stay in the living room and don't go into the bedroom where Nevdra is alone the whole time. Nevdra comes out of the bedroom to ask me where her phone is and to accordingly accuse me of stealing it.

After multiple times of me denying that I don't have any earthly idea of where her phone is, I actually go search for her phone in the bedroom – which is the first time that I go in there from when Nevdra got home because it must be there. I searched for a long time, unsuccessfully. Then I remember that I didn't recall even seeing the phone in her hand – Nevdra's usual habit when she comes home drunk – when she came into the apartment. So, I ask Nevdra if it's possible that she never brought it inside. Since drunk Nevdra is a perfect goddess incapable of making any errors, she won't even entertain the idea. I beg Nevdra to at least go check because I know if I go and find it, she'll just accuse me of having it the whole time. Nevdra won't even look because she swears that I somehow stole the phone from her when she was alone in the bedroom that I hadn't entered until *after* she realized that she didn't have her phone.

Sadly, this isn't the first nor last time that Nevdra has accused me of stealing her phone when she misplaced it when she was alone. A couple of times it fell under the bed and one time she accused me of stealing her wallet in the same type of scenario for that to appear hidden underneath some socks and underwear in her dresser drawer. I guess that she thought that even though I paid all of the bills and paid for virtually everything that I'd still steal from her for some reason.

Anyways, on this occasion I became convinced that her phone wasn't in the apartment so I begged her to at least humor me and look for it in her car. Nevdra not only refused to go look, but started threatening that if I don't give her the phone that she will beat my ass. I begged her and pleaded that I didn't have it, there's no way that I could have it, and to just please believe me. Apparently, getting on my knees and begging her profusely to stop hitting me was not the right move because it just put me in the perfect position for her to kick my head. Luckily, I got my arm up in time to block it, but still caught some damage on that one. I managed to convince Nevdra to let me go look in her car – I know that sounds so sad that I had to get her to agree to let me leave to look, but if I had managed to escape to do it without her "permission" Nevdra would just deadbolt the door and I would be stuck outside for hours – again.

When I went to Nevdra's car, I started calling her phone again and heard it ringing this time unlike when I called from within the apartment. Almost immediately I found it under the driver's console by the gas / brake pedals. Before touching the phone, I took photos of it to evidence where it was. When I returned with the phone and the photographic evidence, Nevdra realized how mistaken she was, was embarrassed by her actions when she's drunk, and apologized profusely for doubting me, falsely accusing me, and beating me up. *Yeah right*! Nevdra grabbed the phone, closed the door in the bedroom, and stayed in there alone until she passed out.

Apparently, that was not enough for Nevdra because on one random day that Spring (March 13, 2023 or so) we decided to take a trip to Galveston. Nevdra had told me that one of her favorite things to do is to go to the beach in Galveston where she pays an entrance at this bar that has a pool in it and can leave her car in their parking lot all day and go to the bar. For some reason, my dumb ass agreed to go do this.

We got there fine and did the bar thing. We didn't hang out in the actual pool because it was full of people with their kids. One group had a Cuban flag and since Nevdra is racist against Cubans, she wanted to avoid the pool area as much as possible. We ordered a pitcher of piña colada or margarita or some similar drink like that. Naturally, Nevdra drank more than I did. Finishing the first pitcher, we moved from the bar to an open table facing the beach. We got another pitcher and halfway through, I ask her "what else do we do?". Nevdra said that this is it – just sit there and drink. I found this pretty boring so I asked if we could do something else. That pissed her off because I dared to say that just drinking at a bar was boring to me. Nevdra complainingly took me to walk the beach. We got into the water for a little bit, but it was getting a little rough so we didn't stay in the water long.

Nevdra then wanted to go to another bar that she likes to go to since it was nighttime. She ordered some drinks and started getting more and more drunk. I knew that this wasn't going to end well so I tried to get her to leave. It got to the point where Nevdra only left because the alcohol was making me sick – it was probably more psychological though if we're being honest. While I didn't throw up, I did dry heave pretty bad. Nevdra was so mad because she couldn't keep drinking that she wouldn't walk on the same side of the street as me on the way to the car. Well, that was after we walked on the beach and she ripped my gold nameplate chain that I've had for about 20 years or so from my neck, tearing the chain in the process. It was a gift from my mother from when I was a teenager.

We finally got to the car and started to drive off when we saw a cop car from a distance. For some reason, Nevdra started honking the horn while I was driving to get the police officer's attention. Fortunately, the cop either didn't care or didn't see us and we weren't stopped. Somehow, we made it home safely.

This time Nevdra at least recognized that she was wrong for breaking my chain and went with me to pay to have it repaired. The funny thing is that when we went to one of the malls in town the next day or so, the random jewelry repair store that she picked just so happened to be the one where her son's aunt worked. Even though she hadn't seen Nevdra in years, of course she recognized her. So, I inadvertently met someone who is kind of a family member that Nevdra didn't want me to meet.

Technically, Summer doesn't begin until the Summer Solstice on June 21st so it's still Spring before that in June. So, on June 3, 2023, Nevdra invited her daughter, sister, and niece and nephew to come hang out by our pool. As I had mentioned before, the niece and nephew are pretty cool. While I hung out mostly with the nephew the last time, I actually ended up hanging out mostly with the niece this time. I hope that I gave her some good advice on the issue that she was having – didn't want to meet her mom's boyfriend's kids because she wasn't sure how she felt about meeting someone new like that. Her parents were married since before she was born and this was the first time since they separated that she was in this situation. I think that she did take my advice because I know that their two families started spending a lot of time together.

I mostly hung out with the children that day while Nevdra hung out with Jackie and Claudia in and around the pool. Surprisingly, we[26] were all drinking (even I got a little tipsy) and no incidents occurred. I think that Nevdra may have talked some shit about me at some point, but I kept my distance from her and her family distracted her, so nothing happened even after they left.

Unfortunately, the same certainly cannot be said about what happened a week later on June 10, 2023 when we went to a club[27] with Jackie and her boyfriend. Even when I was living with my daughters' mother, we never really went out together because the only person that we ever had watch the girls for us was her mother who lived about an hour and half away. Even though she said that she didn't mind, we still felt bad about her driving so we would ask her to babysit sparingly. To recap, the only babysitter that I've ever known or used for my daughters was my former mother-in-law. And while she is a very sweet lady, she loves the

---

[26] Just the adults, not the children

[27] The club was called Se7en in Houston and I can tell you the name of the establishment since it went out of business already.

girls (and all her grandchildren), and I love and respect her immensely, I was not about to ask her to babysit the girls so that I could go out with my new paramour – especially while we were still in the middle of the divorce. And of course I wasn't about to ask their mom to watch them on one of the few days I had with them.

Honestly, I hated the idea of going out without my daughters when I have them to begin with. I felt like I have plenty of time to go out with Nevdra when I don't have the girls. But Nevdra insisted because Jackie's boyfriend invited us to go to a new place that Nevdra really wanted to check out. Nevdra convinces me to let her sister babysit the girls for a few hours so that we can check it out. Guess that her family felt that things had gotten serious enough between Nevdra and me and I was going to last. Thus, it was time for them to meet my family as well. I agreed as long as it was only going to be for a few hours and Nevdra assured me that it would only be for a couple of hours and that it would be good for them to meet what would one day be their aunt and cousins. We dropped them off with Claudia who had a new dog at the time which my daughters loved. It was harder for me to leave them than it was for my daughters to see me go.

We get to the club for a double-date and do the obligatory photographs outside before heading in although it was still pretty bright outside and the way that the décor was set up, it was designed to be more photogenic at night. Since it was technically a restaurant, I assumed that we would basically just have a laid-back dinner and still be able to get the girls in time. But since it was Nevdra, of course alcohol was involved. We all drank a drink or two during dinner, but when we had finished eating Nevdra and Jackie wanted to keep drinking a little bit more. Nevdra kept saying that it was fine and the girls were fine, so another hour wasn't a big deal. So they kept drinking and I kept looking at the clock… And with my luck being the way that it is, the weather also started getting really, really bad.

Claudia did not sign up for more than a couple of hours and I never intended to put that responsibility of watching the girls for more than a couple of hours on her either. She kept calling and texting Nevdra – rightfully so – to see where we were at and how much longer we'd be. Come to find out that Nevdra basically lied to me and Claudia because she never intended to come back after only a couple of hours. Guess that the weather did help us because I was able to use it as an excuse to leave as soon as the weather calmed down. Claudia said that the power went out at her house and when the weather got bad enough to knock over lamps and blow open the door at the club, I used the opportunity to finally drag

Nevdra out of there. Thankfully, Jackie's boyfriend saw my despair and helped me convince Nevdra to leave – by saying that they were leaving too.

The car ride to pick up the girls was absolutely no fun. Jackie's boyfriend ordered my daughters some brownies for them. In the car, Nevdra ended up throwing the brownies at me saying that he bought them because of Jackie and because that was her daughter, she could do whatever she wanted with them because I didn't deserve them. Nevdra didn't care that those brownies had nothing to do with me or her anymore and were a gift for the girls. I had chocolate in my car for a few days after that.

When we finally got to Claudia's house it was super late, but Nevdra was still belligerent drunk. I was so embarrassed and apologized to Claudia as much as I could. But she also looked embarrassed that her sister was obviously drunk and yelling and just being insufferable. It was certainly something I did not want my daughters to see and something that they didn't deserve to see. I probably wouldn't have gotten them at that point except that Claudia told me that they were passed out already. Claudia actually helped me get them into the car while trying to keep them asleep while Nevdra was on her bullshit. Nevdra did not care at all that these were little girls that didn't need to be exposed to this. At one point she intentionally tried to wake them up so that she could talk shit about me to them. She tried to blast the radio, yell, make noise, etc. Oh and while Nevdra hardly ever spoke in English, she made sure that she spoke in English so that they could understand everything that she was saying. It was so embarrassing. As soon as we got home, I carried the girls inside as fast as I could and put them in their bed and shut the door to their bedroom. I just slept on the couch while Nevdra went into the room as usual. It was so embarrassing that I texted Claudia that we had made it home and what happened on the ride. I wasn't sure if I could forgive Nevdra for that one and told Claudia and Jackie so.

When it seemed like Nevdra slept off the alcohol, I told her that she's getting up and going to the movies with us to make it up to the girls. I wasn't asking… To her credit, Nevdra was massively hungover but didn't complain at all and just did it. She fell asleep during the movie, but still didn't complain. Oh, if you're wondering why I didn't break up with her on the spot, it was because I asked my oldest daughter if she remembered anything from the car ride home and she said that she didn't. The youngest never woke up during the ride, so I knew that she didn't hear anything. I'm not sure if my daughter lied to me about not remembering or if she really didn't, but I took her at her word. Otherwise, if she would have remembered any of that, I probably wouldn't have stayed with Nevdra.

You would think that if all you had to do after passing an examination and review of basically your whole life was go to a swearing in ceremony, you'd be relieved. You know, something like a Naturalization Ceremony where you already passed the citizenship examination and your petition for citizenship was approved. Well, less than a week after that drunken shitshow, on June 14, 2023, Nevdra had her Naturalization Ceremony. But, it was SNAFU[28] as usual.

The night before the ceremony Nevdra happened to have a client. As usual, she took that as an opportunity to get drunk after she finished. That morning, I kept calling and texting her so that she wouldn't miss the ceremony. Likewise, Jackie was also calling and texting her too until she finally answered when it was time to head over there. Nevdra said that she was on her way to the ceremony and asked if I could bring her paperwork and a change of clothes. We managed to arrive within a couple of minutes of each other. I don't remember if Jackie made it before or after us, but

---

[28] SNAFU – Situation Normal, All Fucked Up

definitely not at the same time. I walked to Nevdra's car and gave her what she asked for.

Nevdra got changed in the car and we walked together to the building where she had to go in one line and me in another. Guess that Nevdra couldn't handle being in the line by herself because she was so nervous that she had a little "accident" on her white dress that she had changed into. Luckily, she had a spare outfit in the car that was red — so it still matched the occasion (red, white, and blue – *pa' que lo sepa*). She barely made it in time to make the cut-off. Nevdra had to convince the line monitor that she had an emergency bathroom situation. Apparently, the guy was still trying to tell her that she couldn't leave when she walked off. But, Nevdra got changed and made it back. That guy was really confused when he saw her in another outfit. Nevdra went from being in the middle of the line to being the very last person barely making the cut-off. It did look like she wore that outfit on purpose, so it wasn't too bad.

And Nevdra being the last person meant that there was no one in the seat behind her. So I was able to sit next to her using the fact that she was technically my client since I did the naturalization process for her and I asked if I could sit with my client. Oh, and because we weren't together that morning, I was able to get her flowers and a little stuffed USA bear for the occasion which I gave to her at the ceremony. Yeah, I know, I should have been pissed at Nevdra for not coming home, but I put my feelings aside because it was too much of an important moment to not celebrate. Nevdra had her faults, but I was proud of her accomplishing this because she studied her ass off and pushed through her anxiety to do it. But I can say that if it wasn't for me, she would have NEVER done it because NO ONE else would have kept pushing her to do it – even when it meant that she would beat me up. So, when people have told me that they thought that Nevdra used me to get her citizenship, it's certainly not the case.

What Happens in Vegas, Doesn't Always Stay in Vegas

So after all of that violence and abuse, the relationship was long overdue for ending. I mean, unless I'm a complete idiot and decided to take it to the next level instead... If you're still with me by now, then I'm sure that you can guess which option I went with. Yeah, that's right, I bought her an engagement ring, showed it to her daughter to see if Nevdra would like it, and planned an engagement. Her government birthday is on June 18th so I wanted to celebrate it with her. Nevdra's actual birthday is January 18th but back when she was born in El Salvador, her parents didn't register her birthday until June 18th so that's the date that they put on her birth certificate. And if you think that she'd celebrate twice a year, you'd be right! For Nevdra's January birthday, we celebrated on three different days: one day we went to this place outside of Austin that she liked to go to where she got some great pictures of us together and of just her, another day we just had cookie cake and ice cream with the girls who got her some small gifts and a card, and on her actual birthday (a Wednesday this year) I took her out to a Brazilian steakhouse to celebrate.

Around this time, my divorce had settled via mediation so the divorce was essentially over. Or so I thought, but my ex-wife's attorney is either incompetent, intentionally drove up the cost for my ex-wife, or both. I won't say her name, but feel free to look her up. She's the absolute worst attorney that I've ever come across. She was so terrible that the judges felt bad for her and let her get away with things that she definitely wouldn't have gotten away with in a bigger county – it was kind of like how you treat that "special" kid that's "trying their best".

Anyways, I booked the tickets to Las Vegas to celebrate because I've never been before and although Nevdra has been several times, she had never been to the Grand Canyon and always wanted to go. We celebrated Father's Day early and flew out to Las Vegas on Father's Day.

To be honest, I completely forgot that that Sunday that I booked the flights and hotel was the same Sunday as Father's Day until much later.

I didn't want to overshadow Nevdra's birthday with the engagement, so I planned the trip to the Grand Canyon for the day after her birthday. Since going to the Grand Canyon was going to be special for Nevdra, I wanted to make it unforgettable by proposing to her there. I found a Spanish speaking tour that had multiple stops and narrowed down the proposal location to two possible locations. Being with Nevdra all the time on the trip made it a little difficult to not only write what I was going to say during the actual proposal, but to memorize it as well. I was still a little unsure of a couple of words since my Spanish isn't perfect and it definitely had to be in Spanish. But we met some people at a stop that were from a sister tour and I took the opportunity to ask a few older ladies what the proper way to say some of it was. They were really nice. I also told the tour guide what I was planning to see if he could help me out, and he agreed but said that the location that I really wanted to do it – the Skybridge – doesn't allow cameras.

There's a natural formation at the Grand Canyon that looks like an eagle. It's considered sacred to the native tribes there. Perfect! One of the workers there was around the rock and I told him that I wanted to propose to my girlfriend and asked him if it was okay to do it there and after he said that it was, I asked him if he could record it for us. He graciously agreed. Of course Nevdra wanted to take a picture of the eagle, but I was able to convince her that the worker told me where the best spot is to take the picture. When no one else was at that spot, I gave my phone to the worker and signaled to him that when I got back to the spot to start recording. We were standing up facing the eagle together and I basically did the "what's that over there?" thing to get Nevdra to turn around. I dropped down to one knee and when she turned around to ask me what she was supposed to be looking at, I already had the ring out and went into the proposal. Nevdra said yes, and I put the ring on her finger and did the whole kiss / hug thing. Other people were within view of us and saw what was going on and clapped. It was a beautiful moment. We finished the tour and went out to a fancy restaurant when we got back.

We did have a couple of minor arguments during the rest of the trip though. The first was more of an annoyance and Nevdra told me that something was only 4 blocks so I told her that we could walk it. It turns out that a "block" for her was not one street to another, but much, much further. So Nevdra was a little annoyed that we walked, but we kind of laughed about it later. The second was a little embarrassing. One of my best friends from law school lives in Vegas and I thought that it would be a great idea to do a double date with her and her husband, especially since Nevdra hadn't really met any of my "people". But oh no, Nevdra got upset because I made preliminary plans to meet up with my friend without telling her. She accused her of being someone that I had slept with and Nevdra has no intention of meeting anyone that I've been with. My friend was like a sister to me in law school and we NEVER did anything with each other. I was so embarrassed that I had to cancel the plans – she was going to pick us up with her husband and take us to a nice place a little out of town that the locals love that most tourists don't know about – by saying that Nevdra wasn't feeling well. I'm pretty sure that my friend knew that I was lying, but was kind enough to be understanding.

Vicious Verano

It's officially summer when we get back from Las Vegas and we're engaged to be married. We hadn't set a date yet since we had to wait 30 days from when my divorce was final, and we had no idea when it would be final. But, we agreed that we didn't want a big ceremony cr anything where we'd invite anyone because Nevdra didn't want to spend money on people who really didn't matter to our happiness. Everything should be golden at this point...

But it wasn't; Nevdra still got hostile when she got drunk and yet still felt the need to get drunk. Me being a fat kid at heart, Nevdra knew that she could use food to hurt my spirit. Admittedly, I had lost a lot of weight while I was with Nevdra; especially when we first got together. It was a combination of eating less fast food / eating out[29] and all the "physical activity" that we engaged in. We did also go to the gym a little bit and I got physically sick to my stomach for like a week towards the beginning of our relationship. But, I've still got a fat kid soul and sometimes Nevdra would throw away the food that she cooked – often before I even ate any of it – because I guess that I didn't deserve it when she got drunk and mad at me. Mind you, I paid for all of the groceries all of the time, so Nevdra throwing away the food that she cooked actually erased any goodwill that she had with cooking because not only can I not eat the food that she made, but I can't cook it and eat either. So, just an idiotic waste of money.

Now on July 6, 2023, she outdid herself and threw away ALL of the food in the refrigerator. All of it! Eggs, lunch meats, cheese, fruits, vegetables, every damn thing in the fridge! Nevdra wanted to hurt me, and

---

[29] Mostly because we didn't have the money to eat out as much as I used to when I was with my ex-wife and because Nevdra liked to eat relatively healthy and didn't really like eating fast food anyways.

she did. Of course, I was in another room essentially hiding from her when she did this and wasn't aware that that was what she was doing. And no, Nevdra didn't even have the decency to buy groceries to replace what she destroyed.

As it turns out, Jackie's boyfriend has a birthday within a few days of my brother's. So on August 11, 2023, Jackie invited Nevdra and me to help celebrate her boyfriend's birthday. As usual, it was a trendy new place with great photo op locations. At least this one had belly dancers. Not sure if this is what happens during all belly dancing, but this one included dancing with swords and another with fire. The food was pretty good as well. It was a little wrong that Jackie's boyfriend ended up paying at the end instead of Jackie paying, but I wasn't in a place to protest as I didn't want to cause a scene. But not so for Nevdra…

As usual, the drinks were flowing. By the time that it was time to leave the club, Nevdra was already fairly drunk. I'm sure that Jackie was too, but not violent drunk like I've seen her on other occasions. Before we left, a group of Black women came in as well. Since my ex-wife was Black, somehow Nevdra got it in her head that they had to do with my ex-wife. Truth be told, I think that one of them really did look familiar, but I'm sure that I saw her around the law school and certainly not associated with my ex-wife in any way and she wasn't someone that I actually knew. But I wasn't dumb enough to mention that I may have possibly seen one of them, and Nevdra thought that the *whole group* was there on behalf of my ex-wife's behalf anyways. Yeah, it didn't make any sense to me either. Nevdra made it sound like she thought that the women would get together and summon my ex-wife like they were the Planeteers and my ex-wife was Captain Planet[30] or something like that.

Needless to say, when Jackie suggested that we continue the party by going to this hood spot, that I couldn't believe was still open since I hadn't gone in years, I strongly declined. Not only did I not see any point to go anywhere to keep drinking, this club used to be one of Nevdra's spots back in the day. So, the last thing that I wanted to do was go somewhere where I may run into one of her exes. But, Nevdra accused me of wanting to stay at the club to hang out with that previously mentioned group even though we were all outside already, I was going to get my car, and I wanted to go home. I even offered to let Nevdra go with her daughter and her boyfriend to the club while I went home, but Nevdra further threatened to beat my ass when we got home if I didn't go with them to the club.

---

[30] There were five Planeteers who each had a power ring – Earth, Fire, Wind, Water, and Heart – that they could use to summon a superpowered being named Captain Planet when they combined their five powers.

My two options being a sure beating (probably in the car) or going to the club where at least two people may run interference, I drove the four of us to the club. Yeah, that place was just as terrible as I thought that it would be. The kind of place that people our age really should have grown out of going. But we ordered some hookah and more drinks and got a table in the VIP section. Of course, the DJ that night was the same friend that was DJing the night of the first incident that I had with Nevdra. It was really packed, so he barely said hello to us. Nevdra also saw another friend that she hadn't seen in years. I thought that the guy was gay, so I didn't really think too much about it when I saw Nevdra holding his hand when they were sitting down next to me.

Oh, and remember how I said that Jackie wasn't a violent drunk before? Well, that changed. Jackie kind of got pissed at her mom when she saw Nevdra holding that dude's hand and brought up how disrespectful Nevdra was to me and how Nevdra is just a terrible person. Jackie also brought up how Nevdra basically chose one of her boyfriends at the time over her when she was like 16 years old and that's why she kind of ran away and how she never forgave Nevdra for it. Nevdra basically cursed Jackie out and then accused her of stealing her phone. Jackie actually had to be held back from hitting Nevdra. Too bad I let my guard down because when I said that maybe we should leave, Nevdra slapped the shit out of me – just for saying that maybe we should go… that's all.

Somehow, I managed to get them both outside to go before we were all kicked out. Security was already watching us, so it was only a matter of time before we were forcibly told to leave. They even let me go back in real quick to look for Nevdra's phone because they were ready for us to leave. I didn't find Nevdra's phone and they were still going at it when I came back outside. I basically ran to go get the car hoping that they'd be done when I pulled up to the front of the club to let them in. The car ride home was pretty eventful…

In the car, Jackie shifted her focus to her boyfriend and started up with him. I was a little concerned for his safety so I offered to drop him off wherever he wanted, but he insisted that he'd be fine getting dropped off at Jackie's apartment since he had his car parked there. I even said that I'd drive around for a bit to give Jackie a chance to settle in before I brought him back to his car, but he said that it was cool. They both got out of the car, and when they did, I got the gifts that we got him from the trunk. Jackie slapped it out of my hands and walked off. Her boyfriend said that he'd get it from us later and walked with her back to the apartment. I know for sure that Jackie didn't cause him any serious damage or death, but beyond that, I don't know what happened.

I waited until we got home to confront Nevdra on her bullshit. Oh, while on the subject, guess who found their cell phone in their purse? You guessed it, Nevdra's cell phone was in her purse the whole time! As it also turns out, the guy wasn't gay. Nevdra was trying to comfort him because he told her that he had AIDS and that's why he was emaciated and Nevdra didn't even recognize him at first. Nevdra always said that she likes "ugly guys" and has even said "the uglier the better". I reminded Nevdra that she likes to say that and she tried to say that not him though. It was one of the few times that I actually broke up with her.

Before the Next Step

Before we get to the next stage of the story, I thought that I would mention things that happened throughout the relationship or that I don't quite remember when they happened or even in what order they happened, but I remember them happening nonetheless. So, that's what this chapter is all about.

"Good morning my love." Apparently, it isn't cute to say it in the first text that you send your paramour and then say it orally when you first talk to them on the phone. Nevdra told me that it was annoying because I already said it once and didn't need to say it again…

I'm not sure exactly how old our apartment was, but it had this old speaker thing on the wall in our bedroom. Nevdra being the paranoid person that she was, thought that it was a camera and/or audio recorder that I used to record her and that's why I choose that apartment complex. No, not because it was the closest one to my daughter's house that I could afford – it was an 8 minute drive and my daughter's school / daycare were in between it and the house as well – but because I had the painted over recording equipment available in that apartment unit. I don't believe that Nevdra had even finished moving all of her stuff into the apartment when she complained about the speaker. But in an effort to make her more comfortable, I went about proving that it was nothing like that. So, I got on a ladder and unscrewed the speaker from the wall to see what it was. It was there so long that I had to pry the paint off of the edges to even take it off the wall. There were cables still attached to it, but it certainly didn't have any recording equipment attached to it. Rather than leave a giant gaping hole in the wall, I put it back the way that it was. Eventually, the fire alarm siren went off in the building one day and it came out through that box – mystery solved.

Triple crosses on a wall mean... witchcraft? I grew up Roman Catholic, so during the course of doing my First Communion / Confirmation, I ended up with three cheap plastic rosaries. One of them glows in the dark. Anyways, while I don't consider myself religious at all, I did always like having those rosaries as decorations and had a habit of hanging the three of them up on the wall – usually over my bed. Well, in that apartment, I decided to hang them in my daughters' room above the window for no particular reason aside that it was just somewhere to hang them. Well, during one drunken episode, those cheap rosaries became the object of Nevdra's focus. According to her, she looked it up and those Catholic rosaries were somehow used for witchcraft when they were displayed like that over a window. Silly me, I must have missed that chapter in the grimoire because I didn't know that. As usual, I just took them down in order to placate her.

One time Jackie's boyfriend had broken up with her, and he had the misfortune of calling Nevdra when she was drunk. He complained to Nevdra about how promiscuous and unfaithful Jackie is – in more colorful language of course – to Nevdra who obviously already knew all of this but was too drunk to care or even properly pay attention. After that conversation, Nevdra somehow made me responsible for what was going on and blamed me for telling Jackie's boyfriend everything about Jackie. Not only did I have absolutely no idea what Jackie does or know anything about her life, but I didn't even have the guy's phone number or any way to contact him whatsoever at that time. Nevdra ended her accusations by letting me know that Jackie was in need of a new sugar daddy if I was really that interested in their relationship… yeah, no thank you.

Nevdra really didn't like the fact that my daughters used sidewalk chalk on the porch. She would complain that she likes the outside porch area and that it disturbed her peace. I tried to understand how what's drawn on the ground would affect her ability to chill out there, but couldn't. She would ask why I let them "ruin" her space. I told Nevdra that they're just small children drawing outside and that they weren't doing anything malicious. I even had fun drawing stuff outside with them to be honest. And I may be biased, but they drew very well for their ages.

As for the things that Nevdra says when she's drunk, she told me to go ahead and just ignore her. Yup, that's it. Even though I've always heard that people say what they mean when they're drunk, Nevdra told me that she doesn't and that I should not pay attention to what she says and just pay it no mind and move on like she didn't say anything at all.

At one point, I got so sick of Nevdra's drinking that I bet her $1,000 that she couldn't stop drinking alcohol for an entire month. Nevdra's alcoholism was so bad, that either way, I would win. While I figured that it would be "easy money" for anyone to accept that bet, Nevdra declined to make the bet. I guess that Nevdra knew that she wouldn't be able to pull it off.

Places that I've hid from her: in the bath tub with the shower curtain pulled out (that one took a while for her to find me), on the floor in a corner of the room that was obscured by the bed (when she finally found me she said that "nunca te escapara de mi; siempre te encontrare),"[31] outside on the balcony, on the couch with all the lights off covered in blankets and pillows, and what became my usual spot and where I'd go just to get away from her – the spare bedroom.

We talked about having children since she wanted to raise a child with someone that she actually loved – something that she had never done before despite having four children. Well, me being in love, I did think about it. However, I went and "closed down the factory" after my youngest daughter was born. So to have another child, I'd have to get microsurgery

---

[31] Translation: "You'll never escape from me; I'll always find you."

to reverse my vasectomy. Apparently, it is a difficult surgery and very expensive. So before going any further in the process, I came to the realization that we're both older and there's a possibility that the child may have health issues because of that. One of her friends / clients has a special needs child that requires her to basically take care of the child 24 / 7 and getting treatments from Nevdra is basically her only break from that obligation even though the child is actually there the whole time. Nevdra telling me about it made me consider the possibility. So, I mentioned my concerns to Nevdra because I wanted to engage in an honest dialogue about it. But, Nevdra must have already had some drinks in her because she took it the wrong way — basically accusing me of saying that her child would be mentally handicapped because of her even though I said that I was older as well. Nevdra even said that the child should be called "Satan" because it would be the Devil. Needless to say, I didn't get the surgery…

Nevdra saw me playing a superhero game on my cell phone and accused me of talking to a girl on there. She actually thought that the female video game characters on there were real people somehow. Crazily, I don't even use the chat function on any game and it's not like you could tell who was who or what they look like on there even if I did.

It was raining really bad when Nevdra was coming back from work so I mentioned that they said on the news that the weather would be bad so I told her to be careful. This was my response to her when she had sent me a video of the rain when she was driving. When Nevdra came home, she accused me of having a girlfriend that was the weather girl who had told me that it was raining – not the meteorologist, but the weather girl for some reason. And no, I have never dated a weather girl or meteorologist for the record.

I mentioned to Nevdra that I had eaten at the Pollo Campero on my side of town when it first opened. She later accused me of being taken there by some conceptual Salvadorean girl to the Pollo Campero on Nevdra's side of town. Nevdra believed that there was only one and that I couldn't have possibly have gone to one without being taken by a Salvadorean girl (any Salvadorean girl apparently). I tried to tell Nevdra that I actually went with my ex-wife (non-Salvadorean) and my daughter when she was a baby because it was new, it looked good, and we were curious. As usual, Nevdra couldn't be made to change her irrational delusion. Unrelated... well, I guess it's kind of related, the worker that brought our food out that day was a young lady. When she dropped off our food, she asked if we wanted her to hold our baby daughter. Ummm… no… my ex-wife politely declined the offer.

I look absolutely terrible without any facial hair (beard, goatee, or a mustache at least), but I forget after a while. When this happens, I'll eventually shave everything. And when I look at myself in the mirror I'm like "oh yeah, that's why I don't shave everything". I did this one time with Nevdra and when she saw me, her response was "te cortaste el pelo porque esa puta le gusta y te dijo que lo hiciera![32]" No idea who Nevdra could have been referring to when she said that, but I guarantee you that NO ONE likes the way that I look without facial hair. My mom has some weird aversion to beards, but I think that deep-down inside, even she hates the way that I look without it.

"¡Estoy tratando por ti cabrón, ni por mi hijos he hecho esto!"[33] Nevdra said that to me once when I complained about her still drinking alcohol after everything that she's done. That one left me speechless because I knew that it was true. Nevdra even admitted that she didn't even

---

[32] Translation: "You cut your hair because that hoe likes it that way and told you to do it"

[33] Translation: "I'm trying for you asshole, not even for my kids have I done this!"

stop drinking alcohol while she was pregnant. And she certainly didn't stop drinking for any of her exes.

Speaking of exes, there really aren't very many reasons why you should bring them up in a conversation with your current partner – especially if you don't even have underage children together. There really isn't any great reason to say their names either. When your partner brings them up by name, it's usually because they're trying to hurt you emotionally during an argument – and this is undeniably true whenever they compare you to them by saying that their exe did something for them that you don't do or have something that you don't have. One time I even told her "I bet that you couldn't tell me the name of any of my exes besides my daughters' mother because I don't think that I've ever said any of their names and I've barely mentioned any of them to you because I know that it's hurtful." And it was true, she couldn't name a single one, not even my first ex-wife or my son's mother's name.

Another thing that Nevdra would do to try to hurt me emotionally involved social media. Remember how I got most of my social media accounts at her behest so that I could specifically communicate with her? Well, Nevdra would post pictures and videos of us together or even just me and would tag me or allow me to tag her in ones that I uploaded. But, when she'd get drunk and mad at me, she would just unfriend me and/or block me on all of them. Then when Nevdra would sober up and realize what she did, she'd refriend request me again. There are videos and pictures that I liked that were lost forever because she'd not only delete them from social media, but would even delete them from her phone. After losing a few that I really liked, I started to save them as soon as she'd upload them just in case she'd do that again. Sometimes Nevdra would bring up a video that she made of us or a picture that she had that she regretted not having any more and I would resend it to her. Sometimes she'd even reupload them. It was a little embarrassing because people would like and comment on our posts together and I'm sure that at least some of them noticed the removal of those posts. The one that really kind of saddened me was not being able to see the "In a Relationship with Nevdra since _____" because of the unfriending / blocking that she would do. All of this was so annoying… yeah, I know, "first world problems"…

As a licensed attorney, I'm required to take a number of hours of *Continuing Legal Education* every year. I was watching a replay of one online when Nevdra comes home drunk. She sees three women alternatively appearing on my screen discussing the PowerPoint presentation playing and *obviously* accuses me of cheating on her with those three presenters because she was too drunk to see that it was clearly a recorded presentation. Nonsensically, she yells at me that I'm even cheating on her with a lesbian because one of the presenters had short hair…

Nuptials with Nevdra

After all of that, you're probably wondering what happened with the engagement. Well, Nevdra did actually lose the wedding ring – or so she thought at the time. Nevdra had taken it off to go to work and left it possibly on her nightstand, but not in the box of course, because she didn't want to lose it or have it stolen at her client's place since she had to take it off to use her machine. I was really worried that it was my fault that the ring was lost because I had run the robot vacuum in the room when Nevdra was at work and I was afraid that it had knocked the ring onto the floor and then sucked it up. I dumped the vacuum "bag" into the trash so I had that doubt whether the vacuum could pick up the ring and whether I would hear the ring rattling inside the container or see it fall into the trash.

Nevdra did actually find it months, months later, but I'll get to that further on. And when I say "wedding ring", I'm actually referring to the "engagement ring" and not the "wedding band". It doesn't seem to be much of a tradition any more, but you're supposed to have an engagement ring and when you get married, the wedding band is connected to the engagement ring to make one ring set. I had bought the wedding set, but held on to the wedding band until we got married.

As for my wedding ring, I picked the cheapest one that I could online that was still decent looking and sent her the link to it. That was the one thing that I made absolutely clear to Nevdra was that I was not going to pay for my own wedding ring. Surprisingly, Nevdra didn't protest that at all. Not at the time though anyways, but one day Nevdra got drunk and mad at me and was telling me that she wanted this very specific amount of money back that she gave me. I didn't realize it until the next day, but that was the amount of money that Nevdra paid for my wedding ring and that's what she was referring to even though she wouldn't come out and say it and never admitted that she was referring to that.

I got divorced at the end of August 2023. Our state has a 30-day waiting period before a divorced person can marry anyone else. Makes sense since usually the divorce court still has authority over the divorce for 30 days after it's signed. Guess that it helps cut down on any *issues* that could come up. So, I couldn't legally get married to anyone until basically October. Coincidentally, when we had to pick a dating anniversary, we chose October 4th. But, in between getting the marriage license and the

72-hour waiting period to actually get married, we really couldn't do it on the 4th. I thought that October 5, 2023 would be easier to remember anyways[34], so I asked my buddy who is a parttime judge if he would do us the favor of performing the wedding ceremony and he kindly agreed.

So, why did I marry Nevdra? A few reasons actually. First and foremost, I thought that I was in love and she was in love with me. Nevdra would often tell me that I was the love of her life and I believed her. Sometimes she would wait until I was asleep or falling asleep, wrap her arms around me in bed, hug me, and tell me that she loves me with all her heart. I also wanted to be a man of my word, and I would tell Nevdra that I was serious about this relationship and wanted to spend my life with her. I say what I mean, and mean what I say. And lastly, I wanted to take care of her. Sadly, in the US, healthcare is expensive and I had insurance through my work that was pretty good, so I wanted Nevdra to be able to take care of her medical issues that she was having. Yes, one of those issues was going to see about getting help with her alcohol addiction. Actually, that one was probably the biggest one. There's counseling and medication that Nevdra should have been able to receive. Inpatient

---

[34] October 5th is 10/05 so just have to remember the month of October (10) and half that number (5).

treatment, maybe not, but there always hope that she could get that if needed.

Well, on the day of the ceremony, Nevdra was actually really nervous because she thought that she had to write and say her vows to me and wasn't sure what to say. I told her that it would be nice, but she really just had to say what she felt if she wanted to. At the ceremony, my buddy had printed off some nice vows that he found on the internet and Nevdra decided to just use the ones that he had found. She was still very nervous reciting the vows. The vows were in English, but he translated them as he went. But at the end, Nevdra just repeated the last part in English. It was kind of sweet. It was just us since Jackie couldn't make it and Nevdra really didn't care for having anyone else there. There was a small gazebo in the park across from the courthouse so we went there to take a few pictures after the ceremony. My buddy got his clerk to take pictures of the three of us. Again, really sweet and simple.

Afterwards, we went to another Brazilian steakhouse and shared one bottle of wine. It was nice. Just a celebration of us. We had a honeymoon planned, but we didn't fly out for another few days. But we wanted to do something as a married couple. Nevdra thought that we should go watch a movie at the theater together. Figured why not. Here's where I'm at fault though… Nevdra had said that she used to sneak in a bottle of alcohol when she would go with Jackie and suggested that we do the same. I should have known better. Everything was good up until that point. But, I agreed.

At the movie theater we had mixed alcohol into our slushies and started drinking during the previews before the movie started. We were both a little drunk by the time the movie started. Admittedly, we were being a little loud during the previews. But we kind of stopped talking on our own when the actual movie started. Guess that it was a little too late for that because an attendant came and asked us if we could lower our voices. I thought that it was funny because we had already stopped talking loudly, so no big deal.

But nope, not Nevdra. Nevdra took *grave* offense to this. I tried to tell her that it's fine because we were talking a little loud, so we should just accept the consequences of our actions. Wrong answer. Nevdra wanted to leave because she was so offended by the audacity of the people not wanting us talking loud during the movie. I told her to just chill and finish the movie with me. Nope, Nevdra got up and went to complain to the manager. The manager actually gave her tickets to use another time, but I wanted to take responsibility for our actions and I was drunk and my body wouldn't move anyways. Instead, Nevdra got up and accused me of wanting to be with the attendant that had come in to tell us to keep it down. The lights were already off and I didn't even face the attendant when she was talking to me, so I couldn't even tell you what she looked like at all. Logic wasn't on the table for Nevdra at this point. She left and I was drunk and dazed so I didn't get up. I also figured that Nevdra would come to her senses and just come back and sit down with me to finish the movie. Guess I wasn't thinking straight because I was drunk.

When the movie let out, I see the car, but I don't see Nevdra near it. I actually don't see her at all. Jackie calls me and asks me what's going on because her mom is telling her that she needs a ride to leave. I drive around and I find her walking down the street (not towards the apartment or anything, just walking). I tell her to just get in the car and go home. She throws the wedding band on the ground. I didn't realize that at the time. Eventually, I convince her to just come back home with me even though she says that she wants a divorce already. The next day, I had to pick up my daughters for the weekend – another reason why we didn't go on our honeymoon yet – and Nevdra asks to go to the movie theater for the slim chance that we can find the wedding band. We all looked in the parking lot and asked the movie theater people if they found it, but nothing. I hope that whoever found it had better luck with it than we did.

The marriage didn't end the same day that it started, so we did end up going on our honeymoon. The honeymoon itself wasn't that bad. That's probably a little surprising since we were at an all-inclusive resort in Cancun that had unlimited alcohol. For the most part, we just drank piña coladas – a lot of piña coladas. Ironically, I actually got blackout drunk one night – Tequila Night. Definitely turned me off tequila after that night. I threw up when we got back to our hotel room after apparently being a little obnoxious. I thought that I was being witty; I was not. I remember Nevdra trying to say some things to me when I was drunk – maybe trying to start an argument but I was so wasted that I was just apologetic towards everything that she said instead of argumentative. Guess that Nevdra thought that it was her opportunity to turn the tables on me, but she didn't anticipate my reactions would be what they were. When Nevdra told me the next day everything that I did, I just believed her without argument and felt really embarrassed. I didn't do anything too crazy, just said some remarks that came off as insulting to people when I thought that I was being funny, charming, and empathetic. I guess that Nevdra expected me to react the way that she does when she's drunk and the way that she does when she's called out on it. But other than that, the honeymoon was an overall positive experience. We even agreed that we should return one day.

November with Nevdra

Even though we had already gone on our honeymoon, we actually received an overseas trip as a wedding gift. Jackie's boyfriend gifted us a trip to El Salvador, Nevdra's country of birth. Nevdra hadn't been back to El Salvador in like 30 years when she left it as a child fleeing the war[35]. With Jackie and him joining us, he got a really nice, spacious rental home and paid for the flights and transportation. An amazing and unexpected wedding gift!

Everything was pretty good until the first night there… As mentioned before, Jackie also has an alcohol problem – like mother, like daughter. Jackie also likes to take videos and photographs; but she does like to edit her pictures a lot more than Nevdra though. Well, when we were checking out the rental house, Jackie video-recorded the stairwell from the house down to the pool area without anyone knowing. No big deal, but she unintentionally recorded Nevdra going down the stairs when she did that. Jackie uploads the video to one of her social media pages –

---

[35] The Salvadorean Civil War (1979 to 1992)

again no big deal and no one else even knew that she did that. Turns out that this guy that Jackie really liked at the time commented on the video basically asking "who is that" referring to Nevdra. That got to drunk Jackie who has had a complex regarding her mom her whole life. It must be rough to have grown up with the "hot mom", especially one that wasn't loving and caring like Nevdra was.

Jackie got drunk by the pool while Nevdra and me were getting settled in our room and checking out the rest of the grounds. By the time that we went down to the pool, Jackie was wasted and verbally attacking her boyfriend. This was the first night! We tried to get Jackie to calm down, but that just made Jackie turn her attention or Nevdra. It got so bad, that we tried to get the bottles away from Jackie without Jackie noticing because Jackie kept picking one up like she was going to use it as a weapon. I was in a pretty awkward situation because it seemed like Jackie was going to get violent. If Jackie attacked her boyfriend, there wasn't much that I could do. But if Jackie attacked Nevdra, well, I had no idea what I was supposed to do. If it were anyone else, then I'd be free to use whatever means necessary to protect my wife, but it being her daughter, that changes things. The only option that I could think of at the time would be to block the bottle with my arm if Jackie tried to hit Nevdra in the head with it. Yeah, that would probably have broken my arm – I really wasn't looking forward to that…

Somehow, Nevdra and I ended up leaving the pool area to the kitchen area without any violence. But, Nevdra then started asking for one of the two bottles that Jackie had bought and then started accusing me of hiding the bottle when she couldn't find it. Nevdra said that because I used to do it at the house, that I did it here. I actually never hid any alcohol from her in the house – I wouldn't allow any alcohol in the house and I let her know that, but I never hid any that she brought into the house. Can't say that I ever even had the chance to because the bottles would already be opened and Nevdra would just drink the whole bottle before it would leave her sight. I will say that I have found some empty bottles that Nevdra hid – I guess out of embarrassment – around the apartment a couple of times. Nevdra accused me of hiding her bottles because she would get so drunk that she wouldn't remember drinking the whole thing and wouldn't believe that she would do something that she didn't remember. Anyways, it kind of upset me that she would accuse me of doing it in El Salvador. Granted, given how violently drunk Jackie was, if I had thought about it and had the opportunity, it may not have been a bad idea. So here I was ready to suffer a broken arm for her a few minutes prior and we get into an argument because she thought that I hid a bottle of alcohol (that wasn't even hers) because she wanted to get drunk to run from the problem. We slept in different beds, in different rooms that night.

The next morning, we saw Jackie pull out the second bottle – the one that Nevdra accused me of hiding from her – and I thought that I, at the very least, was owed an apology. Why I thought that Nevdra would apologize to me for accusing me of something that I didn't do when she *never* apologized to me for accusing me of stuff that I didn't do, I don't know. Maybe it was the emotions running high, the concrete proof, or the fact that there were two witnesses, but it still didn't happen. Nevdra actually got mad at me for demanding an apology and wanted to leave El Salvador already. The crazy thing was that Jackie and her boyfriend were surprisingly apologetic about what happened the night before and wanted to get past it. I never did get that apology from Nevdra…

The rest of the time there was filled with tension. You would have never known it from the pictures and videos that we took there, but it wasn't a happy time at first. We were still upset with each other. To calm down and get past things, I just walked down to the beach by myself at one point. The volcanic sands were beautiful! Silky and perfect! The waves were a little rough, but it felt good and it accomplished what I needed it to.

Nevdra was still mad at me for the first day or so and still wanted to leave but I told her that we couldn't afford it and that we don't need them to make the most of it. We didn't have a car and even if we did, it wasn't exactly a place where we'd be comfortable driving. I did convince Nevdra to give it a chance and if things didn't go well, we'd get our own hotel until our departing flight. Nevdra agreed so long that if Jackie insulted her even one more time, we'd leave no questions asked.

There were a couple of restaurants within walking distance, so we walked to the nearest one and had a late lunch. When we got back, Jackie's boyfriend asked where we were because he wanted us to go to dinner together. Nevdra was in a much better mood because she didn't want him to know that we had gone to eat so that we could go back to the same restaurant that we had gone to. This time, we got the house attendants to give us a ride. Oh yeah, the caretakers were a family that lived in a house right next to the rental place. I'm sure that they watched us on the cameras the night before making sure that they didn't need to call the police or an ambulance.

Jackie was kind of on her best behavior with her mom after the first night. There were a few sly remarks here and there, but nothing strong enough to make Nevdra *pull the switch*. The four of us went to a few places together that were nice and Nevdra and I just kind of did our own thing when we were back at the rental. Nevdra and I went to breakfast at one of the other restaurants that was really nice. We asked if they had breakfast since it was like 11 am and they just opened and the worker said that he knows that they're working on a new breakfast menu and he guesses that he could ask the cook if he can cook some omelets or something. We told him that we were looking for a traditional Salvadorean breakfast and the dude's indifference to disappointment quickly changed into enthusiasm as he ran to the cook to let him know what we wanted. It was a good traditional Salvadorean breakfast!

On the penultimate night before we left, Jackie and her boyfriend wanted to go to the tourist area to go partying. Nevdra and I really didn't want to go, since we had just got back from dinner by ourselves. They were hungover, and we were starving so we just walked to the restaurant to go eat. Funny story, we realized that Nevdra left her purse at the restaurant when we had gotten back to the rental, so I walked back there by myself. It was sunset when we left so it was starting to get dark on my walk back. I passed by a car that had pulled over on the side of the road on the way there. Then on the way back, it was pretty dark and the same car was parked there. But this time it was so dark that I wanted to stay as close to the side of the road as possible to avoid getting hit by a car. As I walked past the car, it was obvious that the two people inside were hooking up! No, I didn't look inside the car to get a good view if you're wondering.

Well, Jackie and her boyfriend had been gone a while and we were already back in our room when we heard them come in. They were arguing, slamming doors, and throwing things, so we came down to the living room area that was right outside of their room – *just in case*. While we were watching TV, we see a white butterfly fly into the living room and then we hear a loud slam coming from the room. We run in and Jackie's boyfriend has Jackie pinned on the bed with his hands around her throat. I basically bum-rush the guy to get him off of Jackie while Nevdra runs to get Jackie. I throw him out of the room and he walks outside explaining what had happened. I would have never believed that he would get violent; never saw any violent inclination from him. And I wanted to keep him away from Jackie until the taxi – that I had heard him call — arrived, so I listened to his version of the story.

As he tells it, they were drinking and Jackie started drinking with some guys at one of the clubs / bars. Jackie started to publicly humiliate him and then left him to go drink / party with those guys on the beach. He got pissed and after Jackie disappeared for a while, he found her and they rode back together. Jackie didn't stop emasculating him when they got back and even hit him with a bottle – ironic, I know – and that's when he lost it and tried to choke her out. Thank God that Nevdra and I saw the signs and didn't go with them! He said that he would cancel the rental, car ride to the airport, and catch the first flight out of there. He said that he wouldn't cancel our flights because they had already been paid for and he wasn't going to abandon us in El Salvador but just wasn't going to pay for the remaining time there. Fine, that's fair. His cab came and he left; he said that he would send for his luggage later.

He came back a few hours later – like 7 am or so. If I had to guess, he probably went to the strip club that we had passed earlier when he couldn't get a flight. Didn't think that he was coming back, so no one was really watching the door to make sure that he didn't come back. By the time we realized that he had come back, he had already talked to Jackie – and apparently, they made up. He asked for my forgiveness and Nevdra's forgiveness as well. He was genuinely sorry. He didn't really do anything to me personally, but I accepted his gesture. Since Jackie had lost her shoe in her drunkenness and it was a rainy Sunday, the four of us went back to the place to see if we could find the shoe and kind of bond. We didn't find the shoe, but we did get to eat some good food and enjoy the atmosphere.

Given the day and weather, it wasn't crowded and pretty chill. After that, we ran out the clock on our El Salvador trip and made it back without any further incidents.

As I have previously established, I am a proud November Scorpio, and my birthday this year (2023) was a Sunday this time around. Since it was on a Sunday, I preferred to celebrate it on the day before – a Saturday. I had las nenas that weekend, so they had to go back that Sunday night anyways. Nevdra told me that she had a spending cap, so I picked somewhere within those means to go eat. I had my birthday dinner with the restaurant bringing out a piece of cheesecake with a candle on top. Very lowkey compared to my last birthday celebration, but I loved it just the same. Since the restaurant was in the parking area of the mall, we decided to walk around the mall for a little bit after dinner. While in one of the stores, Nevdra saw a perfume gift set that she really wanted. Nevdra's friend had told her about it, and thus Nevdra must have already been looking for it. Of course, when I mean that she really wanted it, I mean that she meant for me to pay for it – on my birthday. That seemed a little fundamentally wrong, so I initially refused. But Nevdra kept insisting and acting like a child until I got it for her. So, I bought Nevdra a gift on my birthday.

The next day, on my actual birthday, Nevdra had a client in the evening so it was just the girls and me until I dropped the girls off and Nevdra returned back from her session. If you thought that Nevdra would at least not get drunk this time that she went out to work on my birthday just because it was my birthday, then congratulations! You're just as naïve as I am!

Somehow, I ended up sitting on the bathroom counter when Nevdra got in her usual violent mood. While I was sitting there on the counter, Nevdra tried to punch me. Not sure if it was because it was my birthday or not, but I briefly experienced "ultra-instinct" when I instinctively dodged her punches automatically. After dodging about three punches, it hit me[36] that my body was acting on its own to protect me – and then the moment that I realized that, it hit me for real. This time the "hit" was an actual punch. When I was living in New Jersey, the tradition was that people would punch you on the arm – one punch for every year old that you are. *Yeah, this was not like that*; it was a legit punch to the face. I try to get away from her, but Nevdra kind of tackles me to the bed and hits me as hard as she could in the head with her cell phone. Not sure if it was the angle, or how it happened, but it caused this giant knot to form where she

---

[36] Pun fully intended

struck me. It looked like a giant balloon bubble. It was a really nasty looking thing. Happy birthday to me!

After my birthday comes my daughter's birthday and Thanksgiving. Despite everything, this would be our first holiday as a married couple. This year, my father's side of the family (my Puerto Rican side) was having a family reunion in Atlanta to celebrate my dad's aunt's 80th birthday. It would also be the first time that Nevdra would meet my mother in person. Since my parents were going to be there, my aunt, uncle, cousin, and my cousin's daughter (who is in between my daughters' ages) were going to meet up with them as well as they live in South Carolina. To be fair, I was on the fence about going and it was Nevdra that convinced me to go. Since I had my daughters that year, we decided to just go ahead and take a road trip.

The trip went as well as you'd expect it to go with two young children. We drove straight there and the eldest daughter almost made it without losing it – almost. She held on until the last hour. The youngest daughter slept most of the way. Now, being on a budget was *fun*. The hotel that I booked online looked decent from the pictures, but it was really hood. It was so bad that the girls basically refused to take a bath there and don't think any of us really slept well that night. The hotel was so bad, that even though it was supposed to be nonrefundable for the rest of the nights, the hotel people knew how bad it was and refunded us the money anyways.

Since we'd be there for a few days, we had planned on going to the aquarium one of those days. I had tried to plan a day for us to go with my cousin and her daughter, but Nevdra took issue with that. She didn't like the fact that I was making plans with my cousin. Nevdra even went so far as accusing me of having something inappropriate with my cousin. She's my first cousin and that would be disgusting! It was so repulsive of a thing to say that I called Nevdra sick to even suggest it! Later on, I wondered if Nevdra had ever done something with a cousin of hers because it was incomprehensible that the thought would ever enter her mind unless maybe it has happened before. When Nevdra did finally meet my cousin, it was a little awkward for me because of what Nevdra said and her disdain for someone that she's never met. But my daughters and their cousin got along great and enjoyed themselves even if it was just at our hotel room where they all came to visit. The best part was my mother, who always likes to complain that my daughters' hair is never "done", thought that she could do their hair. About an hour into doing one of my daughter's hair, my mom was only halfway finished and gave up. My aunt ended up finishing their hair. It was great!

Nevdra did seem to get along well with my mother, aunt, and uncles as far as it appeared to me. She also got along with my extended family – my dad's side of the family at the reunion. Nevdra also did well controlling her alcohol addiction at the Thanksgiving dinner, the 80th birthday party, and even on our one-on-one date night. Aside from her BS about my cousin, it was a rather good family trip together.

Christmas 2023

A few days before Nevdra's mother's birthday (December 23, 2024), Nevdra went out and got drunk and did the whole *argue over the phone and not come home until the next day* thing again. I had decided that I couldn't do this anymore and was going to end things. When Nevdra came home in the morning, she came into the room and woke me up. Before I could say anything, she put her arms around me and said the ONLY thing that she could have said to change my mind. And that was "no se porque hago esto. Necesito ayuda, por favor ayúdame."[37] I can't just abandon someone who asks me for help – especially someone I care

---

[37] "I don't know why I do this. I need help; please help me"

about. So, I told Nevdra that I would help her. My insurance provided alcohol addiction treatment, so we were going to go through them. Unfortunately, it had taken my insurance some time to put Nevdra on after we were married so she hadn't been able to start treatment yet.

Since her mother had invited us to join the rest of Nevdra's family to celebrate her birthday at a restaurant, we decided to just show up for a little bit. Things were a little awkward because it was not that long ago that Nevdra had kicked Roger out of our apartment. Roger had been shot several times and almost killed during an altercation with a friend of his newborn's mother's cousin. Yeah, I know, it sounds like the line from *Spaceballs*. But the guy actually thought that he had killed Roger, and Roger ended up hospitalized being unable to walk from the bullets. After being released, he ended up with us. I didn't really mind though since it was nice to have another guy around. I felt a little bad for Roger because you could tell that he never really had a positive male role model in his life – probably never had a regular guy that he could just talk to. He confided things in me that I know that he never told his mother or even sister. The poor kid never had a chance. Which is why he didn't stay with us very long.

After a few days, Nevdra and Roger clashed as usual and he ended up limping out of the apartment when Nevdra kicked him out. He could have stayed if it was just my decision, but it wasn't. I tried to take him to his baby mother's house, but she wouldn't take him either, so I dropped him off at Jackie's house where he had been staying before he got shot. Roger made it seem like it was cool with Jackie, but it was not. He just so happened to still have a key. Jackie was very surprised when Roger used the key to come in while she was getting ready for a date night. I ended up meeting Jackie's boyfriend that night. Pretty sure that Jackie did not want me to meet him since I knew her *other* boyfriend and got along great with the guy. This guy was about the same age as Jackie and seemed like he would have more in common with her than the other guy. Seemed like a nice guy, but it really wasn't a good time to meet anyone given all of the drama that was happening at that moment. I called Roger's baby momma and she pretty much cursed him out on the phone making it clear that she wanted nothing to do with him. *Clearly*, he wasn't going to stay at her place. But Jackie reluctantly agreed to let Roger stay there temporarily upon hearing the verbal emasculation that Roger got over the phone. As soon as I heard that, I dipped out. Eventually, Roger ended up moving in with his grandmother who was living with her son Hummer and Hummer's girlfriend Genesis.

But back to Alicia's birthday party. While there, we were discussing Christmas plans and how they were going to celebrate at the apartment where Hummer (Nevdra's youngest brother), his long-term girlfriend Genesis, Nevdra's mom (Alicia), and Roger (Nevdra's son) all live – and of course we were invited. Trying to be a good brother-in-law, I went with Hummer to go buy a couple of bottles for the party at the nearest liquor store. It was probably as close to a normal conversation between two in-laws that I've ever had with Nevdra's family. We came back right as the dinner was ending.

Not sure if they were expecting me to pay or what the deal was because they all seemed shocked when the bill came and then scrambled to figure out how to split it. As I had mentioned before, I may be an attorney, but I'm not *that* kind of attorney. You know, *the kind with money*. Working several years at nonprofits tends to have that effect. While on that topic, Nevdra was a little upset that I had bought bottles for the party for her family as she considered them all kind of ingrates that are undeserving of anything from our behalf. But since I had left the bottles with Hummer, Nevdra wanted to make sure that she drank the bottle that I had bought at the party so that they couldn't enjoy it.

On December 24th, 2023 Nevdra and I attended a Christmas Eve party at her brother Hummer's apartment. It was a pajama party, so we actually took some Christmas pictures in fancy Christmas clothes before we changed into our pajamas and left for the party. We wore the matching family pajamas that we had gotten with the girls. We had also previously taken pictures together with the girls prior to this. Before we went, we had agreed that we would just go, make the rounds, eat, drink a little bit, and leave after a while. We even had a codeword ("aguilar[38]") between us that when said, meant that it was time to go with no questions asked.

During the party, I didn't notice that Nevdra was drinking heavily. One of the bottles that I had bought was a Bacardi coquito which was actually pretty good. I introduced it to a couple of Nevdra's uncles (by marriage) that I had met for the first time that night. I actually spent most of the night talking to one of them that was Russian; he was a very *interesting* guy. I was mostly hanging out in the kitchen area with him while Nevdra was in the living room sitting on the couch with her aunts,

---

[38] Spanish word for "eagle" in reference to Eagle Rock where we got engaged to be married.

sister, daughter, etc. I saw Nevdra, but didn't see her really getting drinks. More than likely, those people were bringing her drinks. And since Nevdra was sitting down, I didn't realize that she was getting faded. I really did my best to not give her any excuses to take out any drunken anger on me. Around 1am or 2am (December 25, 2023) Nevdra asked to leave the party. She left the party with about a half full or less bottle of Buchanan's alcohol – the other bottle that I had bought for the party.

Since the party was on the second floor, we had to go down stairs to get to the car. Nevdra had started to go down the stairs when I turned around to make sure that the door had closed. Therefore, I was maybe 5 or 6 stairs behind her. As it had been raining that night, the stairs were wet and Nevdra slipped and fell hard on her ass. I ran down the stairs to make sure to help her up and to make sure that she was alright. Immediately, Nevdra starts saying "*porque me empujaste*[39]" even though I was nowhere near her when she fell. I told Nevdra that I didn't push her down the stairs and that I was nowhere near her when she slipped. Nevdra responded "*si no me empujaste entonces dejame usar tu camisa para limpiarme la*

---

[39] Translation: "why did you push me down the stairs"

cara[40]". At that point I offered Nevdra my shirt where she wiped her face on it. Thinking that's the end of it, we continued to walk to my car.

Nevdra gets into the passenger side of the car while I get into the driver side of the car. When I get into the car she says *"vas a ver que te voy hacer cuando llegamos al apartamento*[41]". I put my seatbelt on and pushed the ignition button on the car when I felt the bottle that Nevdra had in her hand hit me square in the mouth. Immediately, blood starts gushing out of my mouth. In shock, I turned off the car, grabbed the bottle from her, and got out of the car. I smashed the bottle on the ground outside – shattering it. I immediately returned to the car and grabbed the car keys that were in the console / cupholder area of the car so that she wouldn't be able to drive my car intoxicated. When I left the car, Nevdra was still sitting in the passenger side of the car yelling profanities at me and asking where I was going.

Since I was walking with blood pouring out of my mouth, the only place that I could think of going was back to the party. I walked in and asked for a "towel or something" for the blood. There were still a lot of Nevdra's family members at the party when I returned – including

---

[40] Translation: "if you didn't push me then let me wipe my face with your shirt"
[41] Translation: "wait to see when we get back to the apartment"

Nevdra's nieces and nephews. Hummer and Genesis took me to their bathroom sink inside of their room where they gave me a towel for the blood, took my blood-stained shirt (a Mickey Mouse Christmas design long-sleeve shirt with green sleeves), and gave me a dark blue Superman T-shirt to wear.

Hummer thought that my injuries were sustained from being jumped outside. At the sink I was trying to rinse the blood out of my mouth but the bleeding would not stop and I felt my front top tooth loose. I was terrified that I was going to lose my tooth. Genesis informed me that she works for a dentist and that she deals with traumatic dental injuries (her words) all of the time so I let her examine my teeth. She looked at it and touched it. Genesis informed me that she doesn't believe that I'm going to lose the tooth, but that it has suffered significant trauma and is certainly broken / damaged. She thought that at a minimum, I'll need a crown and a root canal because there was trauma to the nerve and that it would possibly become infected if I didn't receive treatment. Genesis also tells me that the gash on my lip is very deep and will require stiches to close up before it will stop bleeding.

After a while, Hummer / Genesis found me an ice pack for my mouth while I sat down on the floor of their room. I applied pressure to my mouth with the ice pack wrapped in the towel while I sat on the floor bleeding. In the hours that I was sitting on the floor bleeding, multiple members of Nevdra's family came in at different times to speak to me one-on-one. At times it was immediately one after the other like they had a sign-in sheet outside the door. Most notably were Nevdra's mother Alicia, Nevdra's daughter Jackie, Nevdra's brother Hummer, Nevdra's sister Claudia, and Nevdra's former sister-in-law Veronica.

Found out that Veronica was basically Nevdra's excuse *this time* to direct her drunken rage as Nevdra blamed Veronica for Nevdra's brother Martin not coming since Veronica was his former wife and mother of his children. And because Veronica was there, Martin wasn't going to come and Nevdra hadn't seen Martin in years. Since the last thing that I wanted to do was talk while I couldn't stop the bleeding, I mostly listened to what they had to say. They all basically said – in some form or another – that they apologize for what Nevdra did to me, that I don't deserve what happened to me, that Nevdra has a history of being violent when she drinks, that Nevdra's not a bad person except when she gets drunk, and that I need to leave Nevdra before she seriously hurts me or even kills me.

At some point, Genesis gives me what I believe is a pill of Tylenol for the pain and a bottle of water to drink it. It took me a long time to drink the water because it was painful to drink and I was terrified that I would swallow my tooth. Afterwards, Hummer and Genesis told me that I should just spend the night there and even offered me their own bed since they said that they wouldn't be able to sleep tonight after witnessing what happened. While I didn't want to spend the night – I was bleeding too much and was in too much pain to sleep anyways – I did alternate between laying on the bed and sitting on the floor. For the most part, I was in the room alone with their cat; he was a pretty cool cat though. But they would come in every so often to check up on me.

After a few hours, I did come out of the room to use the bathroom and sat down at their dining table where Hummer, Genesis, and Jackie were sitting there talking. I was still bleeding and was holding the towel to my mouth. After so many hours that the bleeding wouldn't stop and Genesis reiterating that I won't stop bleeding without stitches, I did decide that I should go to the emergency room. Remembering that I had access to free Urgent Care Centers through my insurance, I attempted to find one that was open. But it was Christmas Day and they were all closed. After a while, I did think it best to go to a hospital emergency room. Unfortunately, by the time that I decided that, Hummer had gotten into an altercation with his mother over Nevdra's son Roger. This affected

Hummer so much that he was clearly in no condition to drive and I didn't feel like I could ask for a ride accordingly.

Since the last time that I saw Nevdra, she was still in my car, I was afraid that she would still be there meaning that I could not drive myself in my own car. Furthermore, Nevdra was calling and texting Hummer, Genesis, and Jackie while I was there. No one would respond to her, so all we knew was that she was awake and still drunk. Moreover, they would not let me leave the apartment for fear that Nevdra would be out there and would physically assault me again.

Around 6am, the bleeding wasn't as bad as before, so I decided to check to see if Nevdra was still in my car. I promised Hummer and Genesis that I would look to see if Nevdra was in the car and if she was, I would return to their apartment. I went out there and noticed that Nevdra was not in the car. When I opened the car, I noticed that Nevdra had also done some damage to my car; the poor car never did nothing to nobody. Nevdra had broken the windshield wiper lever off of the car and ripped up almost every paper that I had in the glove box.

I returned to Hummer and Genesis to inform them that Nevdra wasn't in the car and that I would like to drive home. Genesis had also offered to treat my dental damage at her dental office the next day (when they opened again). I managed to drive home without being able to use the windshield wipers since it had thankfully stopped raining. I doubted that Nevdra would be at the apartment since I knew that she didn't have her keys to enter. Remember how it was a pajama party? Those matching pajamas that we wore didn't have pockets, so Nevdra didn't bring her keys or even wallet with her to the party. When I arrived home, I locked the door with the deadbolt, turned off my phone, and went to sleep with the towel pressed up against my mouth since there was still a little bit of blood coming out of my mouth. It was painful to lay on my face and I had to pay attention to my facial position to be able to sleep.

The bleeding did finally stop after I woke up a few hours later. When I was able to clear all of the blood from my mouth, I saw the damage to my tooth along with several cuts on my face. The tooth was clearly broken with a triangle shaped hole in my tooth.

The Nightmare After Christmas

I was able to sleep a few hours and when I woke up, I texted a couple of people "Merry Christmas" and responded to "Merry Christmas" messages – it was *still* Christmas after all. Even though my mouth was no longer bleeding, it still hurt to open it. So, I didn't open my mouth all day – didn't talk to anyone, didn't eat anything, and didn't even drink any water for the whole day. And if you're wondering, yeah, Nevdra was texting, calling, and messaging me all day long. The messages ranged from "porque no contestas[42]" to "venga a buscarme"[43] Since Nevdra knew that she messed up somehow, she even went so far as saying "mi amor, que pasa?"[44] and "soy tu esposa, por favor habla conmigo[45]." And I know what you're thinking, "wow, did you really abandon her?" Not exactly; I did text Jackie to ask if her mom was okay. Jackie said that she had spoken to Nevdra and that she seemed okay. At one point, I even offered to give Jackie money if she let her mom stay with her since I didn't even want to see Nevdra again. One of the things that I did do was get Nevdra's suitcase down so she can pack her shit and go.

After another day or so, I did finally respond to her constant text, messages, phone calls, etc. when she said "esto es horrible[46]" which got to me and I responded with "esto no es horrible, lo que tu me hiciste es horrible![47]" I told her *everything* that happened. Nevdra responded that she did not remember any of what happened and doesn't even remember

---

[42] Translation: "Why don't you answer?"
[43] Translation: "Come get me"
[44] Translation: "My love, what's going on?"
[45] Translation: "I'm your wife, please talk to me"
[46] Translation: "This is horrible"
[47] Translation: "This isn't horrible, what you did to me was horrible"

falling on her buttock, but felt that her coccyx was bruised / hurt and now knew the reason. Of course, Nevdra kept trying to call me even though I clearly told her that I couldn't talk on the phone because my mouth hurt. She almost didn't even hear what she did because I told her that if she interrupted me one more time, I would stop writing / texting and I'd never talk to her again.

Nevdra begged me to forgive her and not to divorce her and promised to stop drinking and seek professional help to keep from ever drinking again. She said that I was the best thing that ever happened to her and although she would understand if I never talked to her again, she didn't want to lose me and didn't want to end our marriage.

For some reason, I cannot hold hate in my heart. Despite all of the evidence to the contrary, I guess that I just really wanted to believe her. So, I told Nevdra that I know myself – and I'm a very forgiving person and could probably forgive her at *some* point. But I don't forgive her *yet* and it's going to take as long as it takes and I have no idea how long that will be. I told Nevdra that if she really wants to stay with me, then she'll have to accept two conditions: the first is the obvious one where she can't drink another drop of alcohol again and would get professional help – the more time that she goes without drinking, the safer that I'll feel, and the safer that I feel, the more comfortable that I'll feel and the more likely that I'll get to a point where I could forgive her. As it turns out, Nevdra actually had her first virtual appointment with an alcohol addiction counselor that very same day.

The second condition was that I wanted Nevdra to contribute more to the relationship – to show me that she's taking this as seriously as possible. We had previously gotten into arguments about her not contributing or collaborating in the marriage. When I was sitting there on the floor bleeding a few nights before, I kept thinking "what does this woman really do in the relationship – in the marriage?" I couldn't come up with an answer. We're supposed to be a team, but it felt like it was a 100% to 0% split. That's not a team, that's a star athlete and a fan, an artist and a hanger-on, a host and a parasite, etc. Now, it wouldn't be fair for me to expect 50/50 from her either. Even 30% to 10% would be fair. So we decided on a nominal amount for her to contribute to the household / marital expenses.

There was a third condition that I wanted her to agree to – I think by now, you know that I have a thing for groups of three. I asked Nevdra to get a job with a more regular schedule. However, she said that she could make the same amount of money working the way that she works than she would get spending a week at a job working for someone else. At the time, I thought her argument made sense; but I regret not insisting on it now – even if it would have been a dealbreaker. So, we just agreed on those two conditions for me to take Nevdra back after I was done with her.

Before all of this, I checked with Genesis to see if her dentist would still be able to fix my tooth. But, as it turns out, her dental office actually didn't take my insurance so it would be entirely out of pocket. After Genesis told me how much just the consultation would be, I easily decided to go ahead and use my insurance to pay for it. Even though it was considered emergency dental work, the place that I went for treatment couldn't get me in until another day or so. On that day, I was supposed to pick up my daughters for the second half of the Christmas break – got to love the *Standard Possession Order*[48]. Having to hide my mouth from my daughters and then taking them to the dentist where I had to keep the reason why I was there was a little rough emotionally. As you can imagine, Nevdra was on her best behavior and not only took me to the dentist and paid for it, but also distracted my daughters while they were repairing my tooth. I'm sure that the dentist figured out what happened since I told them

---

[48] In my State, the *Standard Possession Order* gives the noncustodial parent the second part of the *Christmas break* in odd years like in 2023.

that my tooth was broken with a bottle and my wife paid for everything while being as nice as possible to me.

Since this was the second half of the "Christmas Break", I had my daughters for New Years Eve. What better holiday to stop drinking, right? Well, at least it would be a good test of whether Nevdra could really do it or not. We went to eat dinner and then do an early countdown so that we could pretend to celebrate with the girls. Instead of champagne, we just toasted and drank sparkling apple cider. Probably no surprise that this was the first time that Nevdra ever drank sparkling apple cider – she never even heard of it before. While this should have been a good start, I'm sure that you have guessed that if Nevdra had kept up with it, you wouldn't be reading this...

Nevdra probably didn't last as long as you would think that she would have. She went to work one time and told me that she had drank a couple of beers that her client that co-owned a convenience store with her husband gave her. That lady would normally give Nevdra a couple of beers (one was supposed to be to take to me even though the one that was meant for me didn't always make it to me). Nevdra tells me that she just had two beers thinking that I'd be cool with it – I was not. I couldn't believe that she still drank ANY alcohol after all that. And instead of being apologetic for drinking, Nevdra was upset with herself for being honest about it with me. I reminded her that she wasn't supposed to drink one more drop of alcohol. This led to me letting her know that no one forced her to accept the terms of our "agreement" and that she was free to cancel and leave.

Somehow, Nevdra made me feel bad about my reaction and instead of me just kicking her out, I agreed to modify our "agreement" in consideration of how she seemed to be taking it seriously when she said that she can't just stop drinking after years of drinking (Nevdra said that she's been drinking since the age of 9 but sometimes she would say that that wasn't true) and that it may be a slow process. At one point Nevdra did say that she didn't even stop drinking for her kids[49] (she's even admitted that she drank while she knew that she was pregnant with her son[50]), so I should be grateful that she's even trying.[51]

Nevdrary Fun

What month comes after January? February, of course! Shortest month of the year, the month that we celebrate Black History in the U.S.,

---

[49] Her exact words were *"ni deje de tomar por mi hijos carbón, pero lo estoy haciendo por ti!"*

[50] Certainly wouldn't be surprised if he was born with *Fetal Alcohol Syndrome*; it would explain a lot.

[51] This is the same conversation that I referenced earlier in the book.

and… oh, the month that we celebrate love and friendship on and around St. Valentine's Day.

Since St. Valentine's Day fell on a Wednesday this year, I asked Nevdra if she preferred to celebrate on the weekend before or on the day of; she chose to celebrate on the weekend. So, we went to dinner on Saturday to celebrate. Of course, we showed up late because Nevdra took her time to get ready because she thought that the restaurant would hold our reservation *just because* – it didn't. I had made reservations for a table inside the restaurant and they gave away our table / reservation after we showed up less than 30 minutes but more than 15 minutes late. Fortunately, they were able to give us an outside table at the same restaurant so we just had dinner there. Nevdra wasn't that impressed, so after we ate, she suggested that we go to a more familiar restaurant. We did, and although that place was dead when we got there, we still had a relatively good time. So much so that I even felt good about giving her the gift that I gave her – I bought her a replacement wedding ring. I was a little hesitant to replace the set that Nevdra had lost individually since everything was unsure after the Christmas Incident, but I took the chance and signaled my commitment to making things work. Nevdra seemed very happy and relieved when she opened the box and saw what it was.

Skip a few days to Wednesday which was actually St. Valentine's Day. Now although we had already "celebrated" early, it was still St. Valentine's Day so even if we weren't going to go out, there really wasn't any reason for us not to spend it together. Well, Nevdra had a client scheduled for that day. I didn't think much of it because she often had clients that wanted her services right before a big date so it made sense to me.

We already had some decorations on the glass coffee table that we had in the living room, so it hit me that I should just springboard off of what was there and make a badass St. Valentine's Day display. I had already bought flowers, balloons, and chocolate so as soon as Nevdra left, I went and grabbed them and started decorating the table. I was a little worried that I wouldn't make it in time before she came back, but I had faith in myself. As it turns out, I had much more time than I needed and much more time than I wanted. Around 1:00 AM, I got tired of waiting for her and went to bed. She texted me around 6 am saying that she was too drunk to drive home so she stayed at a friend's house – on St. Valentine's Day…

Since it was still a workday, I went to work that day. Eventually Nevdra came home and saw the romantic display that was supposed to be waiting for her when she came home from working the day before – on St. Valentine's Day. I didn't take it down, but I obviously didn't leave the LED lights on or the candles lit. Nevdra texted me the following message: *"Quiero que sepas que te amo con todo mi corazón. Te he fallado muchas veces y me odio por comportarme de esa manera amándote como te amo. Tengo tanta vergüenza de mí misma que no tengo palabras para pedirte que me perdones.*[52]*"* It must have really gotten to her, because even after all the times that she's hurt me, this was one of the very few times that Nevdra acknowledged the harm that she's done to me and actually apologized. After a few hours Nevdra then sent me some money to my bank account along with a text that explained that it was my St. Valentine's Day gift and that she wishes that she could have sent more. Granted, it was about the same amount of what she had agreed to contribute to the marital household expenses, but I received it as a gift nonetheless.

For being the shortest month of the year, it sure was filled with excitement. Jackie's birthday is also in February, so her sugar daddy offered to take her anywhere that she wanted as a birthday gift. Jackie

---

[52] Translation: "I want you to know that I love you with all my heart. I have let you down so many times and I hate myself for behaving that way loving you the way that I love you. I'm so ashamed of myself that I don't have the words to ask you for your forgiveness."

chose Dubai since she's never been there. For some reason, he told her that she could take her mom with her. Originally, the invitation was just for her. Then another one of Jackie's friends was supposed to go with them as well. Given the once in a lifetime opportunity that this would be for humble means people like us, I couldn't tell Nevdra that she should just stay with me – her husband. Not that it probably would have mattered since Nevdra accepted the invitation right away without even so much as considering me. But eventually, I was also invited onto the trip. At first, I wasn't even sure that I wanted to go given all of the issues that we experienced on the El Salvador trip with them. But Nevdra did her best to convince me, reminding me that there was also a layover in Paris, France – the city of lovers and we could make some memories together there – and how this is not something that I would ever be able to do on my own. The invitation included paid plane tickets, hotel, and transportation afterall. Well, Nevdra succeeded and I even got psyched up about it.

You know who was not so psyched up about my once-in-a-lifetime opportunity? My job, that's who! Although I did have enough vacation time to cover it, the real problem was that I had an upcoming asylum trial that I was still preparing for. If you've never had any experience with an asylum trial, it is very time intensive and takes hours, days, even weeks to properly prepare for. I would have come back a week before the trial meaning that I would have to do some prep work during the actual trip. Figured that the flights were so long that I could have easily done everything and even do witness prep at night / morning before or after everyone else woke up. Most of my witnesses were in another country anyways, so it also didn't seem like a problem. Unfortunately, my bosses didn't see it the same way and they denied my request to take leave. They did take the time to add the personal touch of writing me an essay on why they're denying my request – it's the little things…

But to be fair, it really was the right decision from their point of view so I don't blame them at all. They had also wanted me to do some things in the case that I didn't agree with, so I hadn't done it yet[53]. In any event, I couldn't go. And by the time that it was for sure that I couldn't go, it was too late for them to re-invite Jackie's friend as she had already made plans. Probably had to line up a babysitter and couldn't do it on short notice. Without knowing it, I also had an unexpected asylum interview scheduled for the same day as the flight to Dubai. That interview took much, much longer than anticipated. So much so, that I couldn't take

---

[53] I never did do those things either

Nevdra to the airport like I had intended to because I would have cut it too close. On the positive side, my client did get his asylum granted.

Nevdra drove to the airport and picked up Jackie on the way. Nevdra ended up having to park her car at the airport because I couldn't take her as originally planned. The flight to Paris, France arrived a little behind schedule and it was colder than Nevdra had anticipated. But other than that, there were no issues. They had plenty of time on their layover to have a nice French breakfast and take pictures with the Eiffel Tower.

Apparently, they arrived in Dubai just fine. But I didn't know that because Nevdra lost her phone right when she got there – at the airport. How did Nevdra lose her phone, you ask? Well, the story goes that there's a liquor store in the airport before leaving the arrival terminal. Nevdra, Jackie, and Jackie's boyfriend all went to the liquor store to *stock up* and while doing that Nevdra put her phone down inside the store and forgot to pick it up because her priority was the liquor bottles that were bravely rescued from the store by them. There were also a couple of bottles of water on the receipt, so at least they remembered that they had to drink something other than alcohol. It took so long to hear from Nevdra after I last spoke to her in Paris that I had to contact the hotel where they were staying to see if she even checked in. To my surprise, the hotel would not even give me that information. Guess that I'm probably not the only person who has reached out to the hotel to try to find their spouse.

I finally found out that Nevdra lost her phone when Nevdra convinced Jackie to let her use her phone to tell me that they had arrived safely and that Nevdra had lost her phone. Jackie only let Nevdra speak to me very briefly and mostly it was through text while they were using the hotel's Wi-Fi. Nevdra was only able to send a few 100 pictures that she took with Jackie's phone for safe keeping until she was able to get her own phone back. It was nice to see everything that I was missing...

I was able to narrow down the store at the airport where Nevdra had lost her phone by getting them to send me a picture of their receipt. Can't say that I wasn't surprised, but I was disappointed when I saw all of the alcohol that they bought. Amazingly, the phone had been turned into the airport lost and found. The airport, however, didn't want to give it to Nevdra because they give three opportunities to unlock the phone, and Nevdra got nervous and couldn't unlock it until the last try. And that was after I sent them the make, model, and serial number of the phone from the box it came in and even sent photos of Nevdra with the phone in her hands. But Nevdra did get her phone back on the last day that she was there.

The trip seemed a little eventful as Nevdra had picked a few places that she really wanted to go to and ended up going to *none* of them – even the one where she made the dinner reservations to before the trip. Jackie and her boyfriend had been arguing and then they had been drinking all day before the dinner reservations so Nevdra decided that she would just skip it rather than risk the high probability of drama that was likely to happen. Jackie did get her pictures there though. Speaking of pictures, the little money that I was able to set aside to give Nevdra for the trip was used on the makeup person for the "flying dress in the desert" photoshoot that was part of Jackie's birthday gift. At least the pictures were beautiful after I deleted an assistant from the few pictures where she appeared trying to hold up their dresses.

On the plane ride home, a person died and was transported dead for the better part of the ride. Of course when Nevdra made it home, she got mad at me for very neatly folding her laundry that I did for her and placing it on the bed for her. Nevdra couldn't believe that I had the capacity to do that just to be nice to my wife that I hadn't seen for a week and thought that some unknown woman came over, washed her clothes, folded them, and then hooked up with me on top of all of that. Not sure where such a woman exists, but apparently Nevdra thinks that I know women that would do all that.

Narcissist Nevdra's Nip/Tuck

From what I have read, it's common for female narcissists to be obsessed with their looks and even be obsessed with cosmetic surgery. Nevdra once told me that it was her thing, and she likes doing it until she can't any more. Remember her completely unnecessary tummy-tuck? Nope that wasn't enough to scare her off of getting cosmetic surgery. Nevdra hadn't gotten anything else done since then, but for some reason she decided that it was time to get some more – even after Jackie nearly died from an infection following her surgery. Their stories alone would have been enough to turn me off of it if I ever had any inclinations towards doing it myself. After the Dubai trip, Nevdra went to a questionable clinic with visiting surgeons from Miami and signed up for a liposuction procedure. This was completely unnecessary and I had told her countless times that I thought that she was beautiful the way that she was and it would be absolutely ridiculous to take any surgical risk for something so pointless.

But this is Nevdra after all, so she didn't listen to me at all. Not only was it unnecessary, but it was upsetting to find out that after all of that time where I thought that we had financial problems, Nevdra had $4,000 saved up and used $3,000 of it on this bullshit procedure. Well, it may have been $4,000 as sometimes Nevdra would say that she got a discount and other times she said that it was $4,000. Since Nevdra is the self-professed "Madre de Mentiras" it's hard to know. And yeah, it really pissed me off because she even broke her promise to start contributing to the household – a promise that was made as a condition for me not divorcing her after the Christmas Eve incident. And yet, Nevdra had money that she could have used to keep her promise and show me that she was serious about the marriage. Yeah, guess that should have signaled to me *exactly* how serious she was about the marriage.

So, on March 18th, 2024, Nevdra scheduled herself an unnecessary liposuction at a clinic with a visiting doctor from Miami. The only bright side to this was that she didn't drink for two weeks prior to the surgery and wouldn't be able to drink for at least a month after the surgery. But again, looking back at it, Nevdra had the capacity to force herself to stop drinking if she really wanted to. During the pre-op, Nevdra took things about as serious as usual and lied to the nurse about never taking valium because she didn't want them to know that she's taken it a few times before recreationally. Thought that was a little insane, but if you can constantly lie to your husband, guess that it should not be surprising that you would lie to your doctor. Stupid as it is though. I know that this is a tangent, but don't lie to your doctors or lawyers; it's pointless and counterproductive as they don't really care, but they can't help you effectively if they don't know the whole story. Nevdra also got mad at me because they had to give her two valiums after the first one wasn't as effective (because she had lied about never taking it before) and I jokingly pointed out to her that "yeah, you can tell that it's starting to take effect" when her speech started slowing down. Nevdra took offense to that for some reason. But that's when they took her upstairs to perform the liposuction while I waited downstairs until she was ready. I then took her home to recuperate.

At some point before the surgery, her son Roger came back to live with us at the apartment after he said that he was completely done with his baby momma. By this point, Roger was almost fully recovered. He had a slight limp, but that's probably going to be somewhat permanent. Since he was staying with us, Roger was home when I brought Nevdra back. The first day Nevdra was basically sleeping in the bed with her Colombian faja[54] on. I was on call to help her get up to use the bathroom, get her water and her medicine, and whatever else she might need. After Nevdra used

---

[54] Corset / girdle that is used post-surgery to keep everything squeezed in

the bathroom once, I thought that she would be passed out for a few hours so I thought that I could take it easy in the living room where I was playing video games with Roger. Unfortunately, the video games were just loud enough so that I couldn't hear Nevdra weakly calling for me. And even though I would check up on her every half hour or so, I missed her calling me and she urinated herself trying to get the faja off. Yeah, that was my bad and Roger and I felt pretty bad about it. Fortunately, I had bought Nevdra an extra faja so she was able to change into that one.

Nevdra being the forgiving person that she is, was still mad at me the next morning. While I was trying to help her get ready the next morning for her 24-hour follow-up appointment, Nevdra started insulting me for not doing something like she wanted even though I was following the directions that were given to us by the doctor. For no other reason than just to hurt me, Nevdra says that her ex-boyfriend knew how to do it right when he had to do it. This was the first time that she mentioned that after previously lying about doing everything by herself and even saying that she had no one to drive her to the appointment after the last surgery that she had – the one where her wound got severely infected for not following the doctor's aftercare instructions. Nevdra revealed that he was taking care of her for the first couple of days until he got arrested for using stolen credit cards. Oh, the same one that she had referred to as her "friend" when she asked me to look up his criminal case when he was in jail at the time. Not that I would have cared if it was her boyfriend or not back then, but it just goes to show that she was always willing to lie for no discernable reason. But, that pissed me off so I told Nevdra that if she didn't want or appreciate my help, then she can do it herself.

Even though I was mad at Nevdra and she was hurling insults at me, I wasn't going to let Nevdra drive to her appointment because she couldn't even sit up let alone drive. So Nevdra goes and wakes her son up from the guest room where he was sleeping and tells him that he needs to get his lazy ass up and do something in the apartment and drive her to her appointment. He sleepily and reluctantly drove her. On the car ride there, Roger confronted his mother, Nevdra, on her treatment of me. Roger had heard her insulting me, didn't like it, and didn't think that it was cool. That went as well as you can imagine.

In the ensuing argument, Roger got mad at Nevdra, left her at her appointment without helping her in, got out the car, and stormed off. Nevdra actually managed to drive home. While I appreciated her son Roger standing up for me, I was really disappointed by how he left Nevdra on her own. Needless to say, Nevdra did not want him back in the apartment. Nevdra stayed mad at me for the rest of the day when she wasn't sleeping. Nevdra even said that she didn't want me to sleep in the bed, not just because she was mad at me but because she didn't want me to risk injuring her while I slept. Although Nevdra was wrong for what she said to me and treated me that morning, I still felt bad for her and obligated to help her. So, at night, when Nevdra was sleeping, I put my pillow and some blankets on the floor on the side of the bed opposite of where she was sleeping in case she needed help in the middle of the night. Guess that surprised her that I would do something like that for her, because she stopped being mad at that point.

The rest of Nevdra's recovery was rather interesting as well. The apartment above us had a bad leak / flood that caused damage to our apartment below it requiring necessary repairs. Since the repairs were going to take a couple of weeks to repair, the apartment complex preferred to move us to another unit so that they could take their time with the repairs. However, they didn't offer any concessions – not even paying for or helping with the actual moving. So, given the timing of it with Nevdra's recovery, it would be basically just me doing everything. And since Nevdra had the apartment arranged how she wanted it, she didn't want to move to do it all over again especially when she really couldn't physically move her body too much. So we compromised where the apartment complex let us temporarily move into their show apartment and give us as much access to our apartment as possible during the reconstruction. Of course, they took longer than they originally estimated and, in that time, my father came to visit for a couple of weeks and my daughters had come a few times as well. What also happened in that time was that Nevdra had gone over 30 days without drinking. Yes, it was because she didn't drink two weeks before the surgery and couldn't drink during the recovery, but I still thought that it counted. So, I even got her a bunch of "30 days sobriety" coins.

La Putina

I'm sure that you know that if Nevdra's sobriety had lasted, then I wouldn't have written this. Since you're reading this, you should be able to guess what happened. When Nevdra was finally recovered, she felt well enough to go back to taking clients. And one of my favorite clients, *La Putina*, was just chomping at the bit for Nevdra to come over for her sessions. *See,* her client, Delia, was a 20 something year old, single Guatemalan immigrant. To give you an idea of my opinion of her; while her name was Delia, I affectionately called her "La Putina". Not proud of it, but I called her that because I combined what Nevdra called her – which was *la Chapina* which is a nickname for women from Guatemala – and *puta* which is …. well, if you don't know, you can look it up.

At one point in her past, Nevdra used to rent a small room from a Guatemalan guy named David who was a bartender at one of her favorite spots. While he had "papers", he usually subleased his apartment to other immigrants who didn't have "papers" as roommates. La Putina was one of those roommates who didn't have "papers" and needed a place to live in Houston while she worked under the table. Apparently, her family and David's family knew each other from back in Guatemala as they were from the same town. So, Delia's family asked David if he could rent to her and look after her. David found Delia attractive and tried to show off by paying Nevdra for Delia's sessions – well, at least the first session. But Delia, not wanting anything to do with David romantically, didn't accept David's offer and paid for Nevdra's services herself.

Since La Putina was young, single, and had no car, she would often get Nevdra to drive her places before or after her sessions. Not only would Nevdra pick her up from or take her to work,[55] but Delia would also have Nevdra take her to eat. Nevdra being Nevdra would take advantage of this

---

[55] One admirable quality about Delia was that she did often work two jobs.

and drink at the restaurants when she went out with La Putina. The first time that this happened, I thought that it was a *one off*. But it kept happening with some frequency. One time, I asked Nevdra why was it always La Putina that she would go drink with and she responded that it was because "ella me sigue la corriente[56]".

Well, of course one of her first clients, if not her first, was La Putina. In my naïve optimism I never imagined that Nevdra will take up drinking again after all of that; it never even crossed my mind. To the people that think that I'm a pretty smart person, my apologies for misleading you because I can assure you that I am not. And when Nevdra took a little longer than she should have to finish working and come home, I still gave her the benefit of the doubt. But when Nevdra came home drunk, it really destroyed me; I couldn't believe that she would do it again! That she would throw all of that precious sobriety away; and for what? Nothing! That really broke me. When that happened, her sobriety was really the only thing that was giving me hope at the moment.

I was transitioning from my job – where it was one of those situations where I didn't feel respected and told them that I would rather

---

[56] Translation: "she follows my flow" or "she plays along with me"

not work there than be insulted professionally – to opening my own law firm. Unfortunately, while an opportunity arose while Nevdra was in Dubai and this was in the works, I had needed a little more time to have everything set up for a smoother transition. I had originally given my employer my notice of resignation with a last day after my two upcoming asylum trials in a couple of months. But after another disagreement, they decided to accept my resignation immediately and had me pack up my shit and leave that day. They even told my clients before they told me. That was pretty low to have to answer calls from my clients crying and begging me not to abandon them because I had abruptly quit – which I did not do. Ironically, I might have abruptly quit if it weren't for wanting to do right by my clients. So, yeah, they lied to my clients about what was going on.

I was feeling pretty down and was holding back depression as best as I could. I know, our society expects men to suffer in silence, so that's what I was trying to do. And I basically saw Nevdra's sobriety – the one positive thing that provided me infinite hope – as my anchor. So, when Nevdra came home drunk, she broke my illusion of trust and my hope for the future, and I was devastated. And worse of all is that Nevdra didn't seem to care. Nevdra went from saying that she wasn't drunk because she only had *one drink* to saying that she couldn't be drunk as she only had a *couple of drinks* and it takes a lot more for her to get drunk than she drank that night. But, after all of my experiences with Nevdra, if there's one thing that I became an expert on, it's recognizing when she was drunk. It didn't matter how much she drank that night with La Putina, Nevdra was drunk. And all because she wanted to have a good time with La Putina.

Now that night, Nevdra didn't get the chance to do anything to me as I locked myself in the guest room for a few *days*. The guest bathroom connected to that room so I locked both the bathroom and the guest room and just stayed in there a couple of days. Nevdra blamed me for having to miss a few appointments because she couldn't get into that closet where some, but not all, of her clothes were. Nevdra had probably less than half of all her clothes in that closet so she easily could have found clothes to wear from our closet. Yeah, I wasn't buying that excuse.

The Nevpire Strikes Back

On that night that Nevdra returned to the bottle, she didn't have the chance to return to her violent ways. But that was just that night. Nevdra has been physically violent several more times after *La Otra*[57] returned. For instance, on April 27th, 2024. On that date, Nevdra came home drunk

---

[57] *La Otra* translates to "The Other" which is what I called the person that Nevdra becomes when she's drunk

as usual. In the ensuing argument, she repeated the impressively heartless opinion that what she did to me "eso fue el año pasado, no te hecho nada este ano.[58]" See to Nevdra, her brilliant solution to making sure that she didn't physically assault me anymore wasn't to just keep her promise to never drink again and get professional help to do so – nah, that would have been too easy – instead her solution was to just straight up not come home when she drank. Brilliant, right?

Nevdra came home drunk from going out to work just as she used to before. She again tried to say that she wasn't drunk because she had only had a couple of drinks, but she was drunk. Since Nevdra convinced herself that she wasn't drunk and I wasn't buying into her lie, she decided to get drunk "for real". But since I had given my word that there will be no alcohol at the house, the only alcohol in the house was a bottle of champagne that she had brought back from Dubai as a souvenir. I didn't expect that she would ever open it; or at least not open it that soon. But Nevdra went for it and even taunted me with it. Even though she had that *very convincing argument* that she hadn't hit me with a bottle this whole year, I told her that I wasn't going to give her the chance. I grabbed the

---

[58] Translation: "That happened last year, I haven't done anything to you this year"

bottle and went to throw it over the balcony. Before I was able to throw it, Nevdra tried to stop me by grabbing my shirt from behind. In doing that she ripped my shirt. But I was undeterred and threw that sumabitch as hard as I could over the balcony. I didn't know it at the time, but apparently it didn't break. Guess that it went through some tree branches on the way down which softened the blow enough to not break the bottle.

The other thing that I didn't realize at the time was that Nevdra left a deep gash on my back shoulder blade. I found out after I saw a long line of blood when I woke up in the morning on the pillow that I had slept on and saw it in the wound in the mirror. Instead of taking responsibility for it, Nevdra tried to claim that I scratched myself. And when I demonstrated that it would be physically impossible to reach that angle, she then conjured up a magic knife that would have allowed me to cut myself in a manner that would normally be physically impossible for a person to do with a regular knife.

Yeah, Nevdra is a coward. Everyone makes mistakes and everyone fails, but to never admit your mistakes or apologize for your actions is just cowardice. Pretending that you have no weakness doesn't make you strong; on the contrary, it makes you look weak and pathetic. Nevdra wanted me to accept explanations, actions, and behavior from her that she would NEVER accept from me or anyone else. And when she did it, I would ask her if it would be okay for me to do that; if that'd be acceptable if it were me that did it. Nevdra would tell me that she's going to see a client, then instead of coming home after she was done with the work, she would drink with that client – whom I've never met, then show up drunk or spend the night over there without so much as letting me know where she was or what she was doing or that she wasn't coming home. I saw it as a lie, a betrayal every time she did it. "If I were to go to work, stay drinking with my client, get so drunk that I wouldn't even come home until the next day, and not even tell you, would you accept that from me?" We all know what her answer to that question would be, but she was too much of a coward to ever answer me.

Oh, and this is the same person who would accuse me of cheating on her if I took longer than 5 minutes to go anywhere than it should have. When I was trying to set up my law firm, I had to meet up with my managing paralegal at the bank to open up the business account. Nevdra hadn't met her before this point, so I invited her to come and Nevdra said that she didn't feel like it. So, I went to the bank and came right back home. Nevdra didn't believe that I even went to the bank because I took too long. Doesn't matter that the bank was at least 30 minutes away each way and the appointment took about a half hour by itself. I was so tired of her not believing me, that the next day when we had to go somewhere, I drove her to the bank to show her exactly how far it was and how long it took to get there. Oh, and since I was always everywhere that I said I was, I told Nevdra that if she really didn't trust me, then she's free to use a family location tracker. I've never used one, but Nevdra uses one with her daughter Jackie. Now that would mean that her phone's location would be available to me as well – not that I wanted to track her, but the app works both ways. For some reason, Nevdra didn't want to do it.

When One Door Closes, Another One Opens

Nevdra had a problem with the paralegal that I was opening the law firm with. But, I literally could not do it without her. See I had worked together with her for a few years about a decade ago when we both worked for the same attorney. To avoid confusion, let's just call her Maya[59]. We did end up dating for a few months about 10 years ago, but after we broke up, we remained friends and professional acquaintances. You know on job applications where you have to put professional references? Maya was usually one of my three references since we had worked together and had

---

[59] "Maya Fey" is a character from the "Phoenix Wright" series that was basically his paralegal.

known each other for years. Since we broke up, we have both gone on to several relationships with other people, marriages, and I even had two other kids – and we have never tried to get back together. So, we had years to do it and never did it because neither of us saw each other that way anymore. We were good friends before we dated, we dated, it didn't work, and we went back to being friends after that. But even when we worked together, Maya would always joke with me that I should open up my own law firm because she thought that I was a much better attorney than the one that we worked for and an honest, trustworthy person. And she would always joke that I should hire her whenever I finally did it. Now on her end, I thought that she was very knowledgeable and always trusted her experience and opinions. Always thought that Maya should have gone to law school, but she never did.

When Nevdra was in Dubai, Maya had randomly recommended me to her friend who was having an immigration issue in the same area that I had basically become an expert in. So, she asked if I could meet up with her friend to give her a legal consultation. I normally didn't take cases outside of my job, but from what little information that I had, it didn't seem like she really had a case, so I figured that it wouldn't be a big deal to talk to her. Since I couldn't meet with her friend at my office and I didn't have any other place that I could meet her, Maya suggested that we meet at her home office in her fiancé's house. Didn't see any issue with that – especially since her fiancé would be there. I did the legal consultation and afterwards Maya jokingly repeated that I should open my own law firm. At that point, I had been having a lot of issues at my job, and was already seriously considering quitting, so I figured, "you know what, why not?!" The two things that had always prevented me from opening my own office were a lack of funds and a source of clients. Maya actually had both of those and thought that she'd rather work with me at a law firm where she would make a lot more than where she was working at and her fiancé would gladly lend us the startup money for the law firm. It was more of a rough idea than a concrete decision at that point, but it seemed more and more promising the more that I considered it. Couldn't discuss it with Nevdra since she still didn't have her phone and it wasn't anything beyond an idea at that point anyways.

Unfortunately, I had one of those situations at work where they wanted me to do something and I was like "nah, you know what? I won't be doing that. And if you want me to do that, then I think that our time together has come to an end." Having this to fall back on, certainly helped me make that decision. So, I decided "let's do this" on opening the law firm and started the process. Since Nevdra let me pay for everything, Nevdra really couldn't complain how I made the money. Maybe I was still a little upset with her about not even trying to contribute to the household expenses like she promised to do and be an actual partner in the marriage, so it was kind of like the sentiment in the movie *A Few Good Men* when Colonel Jessup said "I have neither the time nor the inclination to explain myself to a man who rises and sleeps under the blanket of the very freedom that I provide, and then questions the manner in which I provide it!"

Knowing how irrationally jealous Nevdra is, I omitted the fact that Maya and I had briefly dated almost a decade ago because I really didn't have any other options when it came to not going bankrupt. Maya also thought it best not to mention the fact that we had briefly dated a decade ago because it really didn't matter and had nothing to do with the business. And in all honesty, when we actually started our business venture, our friendship changed into a strictly business relationship. The idea was that we were sure that it'd eventually come out, but at that point it wouldn't matter because it would be clear beyond a shadow of a doubt that we had absolutely no interest in each other aside from business interest.

Well, Nevdra kept asking about it, so I eventually told her. Even though it really shouldn't have mattered, I still felt bad about lying about it and I felt that I should have been truthful from the start even though I knew that Nevdra would say "no" to going into business with Maya and we'd be left with no real financial options. So yeah, even though Nevdra would do nothing but lie to me and for her own personal benefit and my detriment, I still felt bad about lying to her one time for our benefit. Pathetic of me, I know. The reveal went about as well as you'd think that it'd go. It also didn't matter that Nevdra was supposed to use one of the spare offices there to work from and that she would be there the whole time.

So, to please Nevdra, I had to end the business relationship which resulted in a substantial loss. So much so that I really couldn't continue the business on my own. Nevdra was supposed to help, but aside from learning how to turn on the laptop that I got her, she didn't do much to help the business. While looking for ways to help her son, I suggested that maybe he should be the receptionist because he's a good-looking kid who could easily get female attention. I figured that maybe he'd be good with the female clients. Oh no, Nevdra took it as I was trying to prostitute her son. Somehow playful banter and light flirting *has to* result in sex according to Nevdra. At one point, Nevdra even offered to contribute

$1,000 to the household bills. I didn't even raise an eyebrow as I wouldn't believe it until I saw it. And no, Nevdra never did manifest that money.

Getting paying clients proved to be a lot more difficult than I had anticipated. And with limited funds to fall back on, and basically no safety net, I went to look for options to stay afloat. I thought that maybe I could find contract work or even a part time job until business started picking up. While doing that, I was contacted by a law firm about 2 hours away that was interested in starting up an immigration division and needed an attorney to helm it. Never considered moving, but I interviewed anyway and they made me a very generous offer at the end of the interview.

As this was a huge decision, I would only do it if it was a family decision with Nevdra. The biggest reason that I didn't want to move was that I would be 2 hours away from my daughters and I hated that idea. But when I discussed it with Nevdra, she thought that it was the best decision for us and even suggested that it may be good for her drinking problem to get away from everyone in town – especially her own family. That kind of really sold me as it was a way for us to start fresh; a new beginning. I told Nevdra that I'm only going to do this if she was 100% on board with this decision and that she'd have to get professional help for her alcoholism – even if it meant in-patient treatment and that we'd get marriage counseling as well. With the amount of money that I'd be making compared to what I was making, I told her that she didn't have to work while she was getting treatment and that she can take her time to establish a business there. Nevdra agreed and we went together to meet the other members of the new law firm and apartment hunting in the new town. We agreed on which apartment we wanted, signed the lease, and worked towards starting our new life together away from all of the drama and bad influences on her.

Or so I thought…

El Que Te Amaba; Lo Que Te Di[60]

After moving everything aside from the furniture out of the law firm, giving notice of terminating our current apartment lease, negotiating a move in date with the new apartment, etc, it was time for me to start the new job. Because of the move out date on the current apartment, Nevdra thought that it didn't make much sense to move into the new apartment while we were still paying a whole month for the old apartment. Made sense, so I decided to just commute for the first two weeks of my new job.

---

[60] "El Que Te Amaba" and "Lo Que Te Di" are two songs by Marc Anthony, translated as "The One Who Loved You" and "What I Gave You" respectively. Thought that Marc Anthony would be appropriate to convey the end of the relationship since "our song" was "Vivir Lo Nuestro", another song by Marc Anthony (and La India), but I couldn't decide which one to use, so I used both.

Yup, 2 hours in the morning and 2 hours in the evening. But it was a sacrifice that I was willing to make for *us*.

I was going to start my new job on a Monday, so I wanted to get a good night's sleep on the night before, a Sunday (June 24th, 2024). Nevdra had a client in the afternoon, so she was going to do that. But the appointment was at 3pm, so even if she did 2 hours, she'd still be back rather early. Nevdra even suggested that when she got back, we could move out a few more things from the law office or even go to the pool together. It sounded lovely to me. I even cooked dinner so that she would have food when she came back. I also received the news that my client from the asylum trial that I had issues with my job over the way that I was handling it, was granted. We had won! I basically risked everything to do it my way, the way that I knew that I could win, and it paid off. That judge granted less than 2% of all asylum claims, and despite everyone more worried about setting up an appeal than actually winning it, I pulled it off. So, yeah, I was overjoyed and couldn't wait to share the news with my wife!

And then it was 5pm and I haven't heard anything from Nevdra. No biggie, I'm sure that she probably started a little late; so she should be on her way soon. And then it was 6pm, and nothing. Surely, I didn't have anything to worry about. I mean, there's no way that Nevdra would do what she used to do the last night before starting our new lives together. She knows how important this last night would be for us together and she wouldn't sabotage this for me and for us. Nah, there's no way... right? Right? Then 7pm hits, and I texted Nevdra to see where she's at – something that I didn't do after Nevdra went off on me early on in the relationship because she didn't like the *pressure* of me checking up on her. No response. I call and of course Nevdra has never cleared her voicemail, so can't leave a voicemail when she doesn't answer.

I call and call until she finally answers. I hear another female voice in the background and Nevdra's obviously drunk. I ask her what the Hell is going on and who the fuck she's with. Nevdra gives some incoherent drunken response and hangs up. Never answers the phone again but responds to text. I ask if she's with La Putina and she halfway admits it. So, after Nevdra made me cut all ties with a business associate, she goes back to the ONE client that we've argued about; the ONE client that has caused problems in our relationship. Basically, Nevdra said "fuck you" to me and "fuck you" to the relationship and the marriage. The betrayal that I felt at that moment was so much that I just turned the phone off and went to sleep – well, I tried to anyway. I really didn't sleep that night and I had to wake up early for my long drive. But Nevdra obviously couldn't care less; she couldn't' give a flying fuck.

The next day I started to argue with her over text, but then I realized that *why should I care anymore* when she obviously didn't. I realized that Nevdra threw our relationship and our marriage in the garbage to go drink with La Putina. There were several times when I told her that it was the alcohol or me, and Nevdra had clearly chosen the alcohol. It was obvious when Nevdra came home because she kept calling me and texting me where I was. Yup, Nevdra completely couldn't be bothered to remember that I was starting the new job that was supposed to change our lives together. Nothing like your drunk wife calling and texting you all day after a long ass drive with virtually no sleep on your first day – perfect start to a new job.

Nevdra must have gotten a few hours of sleep, because she seemed to remember where I was and seemed to realize that she fucked up. Nevdra acted like it was going to be like the other times when she can just get me to move on from being pissed at her. Nevdra kept asking what time I'd be home because she was hungry. ¡*Descarada*![61] Guess that she expected me

---

[61] Translation: "Shameless"

to either pick up some food, go out to eat together, or me make her my expert level Korean ramen that she loved. Nah, I was too disgusted to even look at her. The thought of looking at her, let alone talking to her, made my stomach hurt. So when I got home, I just made myself a sandwich, ate the sandwich, washed my plate, and pretty much just went to sleep. I didn't even acknowledge her. The next day, I left before Nevdra woke up and she later texted me some random question, but I didn't even respond to that. Came home and still couldn't look at her. I tried to play video games and she asked me if we could talk, but I physically couldn't do it. I just kept playing video games without even looking at her. Nevdra quietly went back into the room. I didn't talk to her for about a week; I found her revolting. I was too hurt.

At the end of the week, my daughters stayed with us for the weekend. Nevdra was cordial enough with them during that time even though we barely spoke to each other. I slept on the couch and pretended that I had just gotten to the couch when the girls would wake up. Things being the way that they were, I told the girls the last day before they left that if there was anything that they would want to tell "Elsa" as if they might not see her for a long time, that they should tell her now. My oldest said "I don't have anything to say to her."

One of those days after that, Nevdra said that she had found an apartment to move out to. Didn't think that no one in their right mind would rent to her given her rental and credit history. A few days later, Nevdra said that she had been approved. But given her history of lying and that she hadn't packed a damn thing, I didn't believe her. I did tell Nevdra that although I was pissed at her, that I was still willing to go along with our original plan and work on our marriage in the new town together. For one thing, I never would have taken that job if it wasn't a joint decision by us as a married couple. And by then everything was already in motion so there was no turning back.

Two nights before the weekend – a weekend when I was going to have my daughters – Nevdra was drunk at the apartment when I came home from work. Nevdra said that she got drunk at home because she just didn't care anymore. I went ahead and locked myself in the other bedroom as I had grown accustomed to when she was drunk and went to sleep. After I fall asleep, Nevdra wakes me up by knocking on the door. Through the door, Nevdra asked me if I wanted to have sex. Getting woken up with that question after two weeks of not having anything, made me use a different part of my brain and I went out to meet her. She was topless with pajama pants on. She was still drunk and while I wouldn't sleep with her or anyone else when they were drunk, the thought did cross my mind. I had a feeling that this may be the last time... Nevdra starts saying something stupid and I tell her that I only came out because she said that she wanted to have sex. Nevdra then asked me "que me vas a dar?[62]" I just shake my head, tell her goodnight, lock myself back in the room, and go back to sleep.

The next day I tell Nevdra that she was so drunk that she probably doesn't even remember what she told me – something really ugly. Nevdra asked me what she said and I tell her, and she says that she remembers telling me that. That night I sleep on the couch and Nevdra wakes me up to tell me that she's moving out. Not only is this about a week before the new apartment is ready, but she has yet to pack a single thing. Nothing has been moved at all. While half asleep, I tell her to not move out (still didn't believe her that she had found another apartment to move to) and just keep the original plan that we had – a plan that we came up with as a family. Nevdra doesn't really say anything so I just roll over and close my eyes to go back to sleep. I know that she stayed in the chair next to me for

---

[62] Translation: "What are you going to give me?"

a while just watching me try to go to sleep and then left to the room without saying another word.

The next day Nevdra calls me a few times, but I was legitimately in a legal consultation with a potential client and didn't have my phone on me. She leaves me a voicemail – which she never does – saying that she just wanted to say goodbye to me. Confused, I call her back and Nevdra tells me that she wanted to let me know that she was moving out but has already gotten most of her stuff and will be back for the rest and to help me clean up the apartment. When I finally came home, I walked into a mostly barren apartment. Nevdra not only took all of her furniture, clothing, decorations, etc, but she took pretty much anything good that we had. It was pretty shocking to see that. We had a wall with maybe 30 of our pictures on it and she took all of the pictures of just her and left all of the pictures of us. She even took all of the toilet paper in the house and all of the pots and pans (including the ones that I brought with me when I moved in) because she could give a rat's ass if I had the means to take care of myself. For weeks, I would keep finding out that Nevdra must have taken something new that belonged to me when I went looking for something that I should have had, but wasn't where it should have been.

When going through the stuff that Nevdra took, I saw that she left a gift. Not a gift from me, but a gift from my daughters. For her birthday a few weeks before, I took my daughters to the mall where they wanted to make Nevdra a stuffed animal. They lovingly looked through the store to find something that they thought that she would like, stuffed it, and dressed it. They even took the time to color the box as carefully as possible with each coloring half of the box. They wanted to give Nevdra a good birthday gift and were excited to give it to her. I even took videos of them during the process. When they gave it to Nevdra, she barely thanked them. Afterwards, Nevdra complained that *why would we think that she would like that*. Why didn't we get her a purse or nice outfit, etc. I told her because they were little girls and they got her what they would like for someone to get them.

This is the same person who told me "how would you like it if she had gotten me the same gift for Father's Day that I got her for Mother's Day". I had made her a photo plaque of her children (the two that she claims anyways) and grandson that took hours to scourer all of her social media pages (including old ones that she doesn't have access to), her daughter's social media pages, and other family members social media pages to then compile, edit, and organize the pictures that I found. I told her that I would love it if she put that kind of time and effort into a gift for me and it would mean a lot. Fitting that the last pictures that we took together were on Father's Day when she took me out to dinner and basically threw $20 at me to help me pay for the dinner. But, when I saw that Nevdra had taken everything that was important to her, and left that gift, that took away any sadness that I had and converted it into disgust. I even told her to not worry about coming back to the apartment to clean or anything because I don't want to see her again…

Nevdra No Esta, Nevdra Se Fue

Nevdra tried to tell me that she didn't mean to leave that gift behind and that she even left a gift from her son – which meant the same to her. Rather than believe that Nevdra was an absolutely terrible human being, I choose to believe her. Did I actually believe her though? I don't know. But one thing that I do know is that one of the things that Nevdra took with her was the nightstand next to my side of the bed that was full of my stuff. I had my important information in there in one drawer and ALL of my underwear in the other drawer. Nevdra claimed that Jackie took that without looking in the drawers – and Nevdra claimed that Jackie was the one that selected all of the pictures to take and which ones to leave. As much as I had no interest in really seeing Nevdra, I did need my underwear. The only ones that I had were what were in the laundry – so not much.

It was also Fourth of July weekend and I had my daughters for the holiday weekend, so I didn't really want for Nevdra to come over while they were there. I did offer Nevdra the chance to say "goodbye" to them since it would be what I would want if I was in her situation, but Nevdra declined. I even said that she can come get them on her own without me, but she said that maybe some other time. There was also a hurricane coming towards us around the end of the holiday weekend. Nevdra liked to drink bottled water, and being the attentive husband that I was, I had already at the apartment a full, unopened 24 pack while still having half of another pack. Since Nevdra still had a lot of stuff there – including the water bottles, I had originally told her that she could come pick up the rest of her stuff while I was at work on that Tuesday. But then when it became pretty clear that we had a good chance of being hit by the hurricane, I told her that she could come before then while I was there with the girls to come pick up her stuff and pick up the water. Nevdra wasn't even aware that there was a hurricane headed for us. And of course, she didn't plan for it or come to grab the water bottles. And the hurricane did hit us. We lost power for a few days. One of those nights, I handwrote Nevdra a 12 page letter by candlelight while sitting outside in the apartment. It was a goodbye letter that left the door open for her to still join me on the move which would be about a week later.

Nevdra did come get the rest of her stuff and drop off my underwear and important papers while I wasn't there, but didn't finish grabbing all of her stuff. So, I packed up the apartment and moved without her. I left the few small things that she didn't take with her in the office and told her to pick it up there. Even though she picked up some of that stuff from the office one day, she still didn't get everything. Part of me thinks that Nevdra was intentionally leaving stuff to keep some sort of tie with me. Nevdra also wouldn't return the keys to either the apartment or office which she knew that I had to turn in.

I'm not sure what Nevdra was thinking, but whatever it was, wasn't rational. Her friends that I talked to after the break up think that she thought that I would chase her and beg her to come back. That she's used to toxic relationships like that where Nevdra can get away with anything and the guy will beg her. *No*, she was the one that threw the relationship away, so it was up to her to chase me and beg me to forgive her. Nevdra even did the block and unblock thing to me on social media. She unfriended me a long time ago, but would post things to try to get my attention. One time Nevdra posted something a little bit on the vulgar side, and I thought to myself "why am I doing this to myself? I don't need to see this or what she's up to." So I blocked her on everything. And best believe that she noticed because on July 14, 2024, I had 47 new messages from Nevdra with the first one asking why I blocked her and then accusing me of doing it so that I can post stuff with other women without her seeing it. Those 47 messages were all unanswered and during the night while I was asleep. I was actually a little concerned because it seemed a little psychotic to me.

On Wednesday, July 24th, 2024, I asked Nevdra again to leave the keys and for her forwarding address. I was planning to come back into town to finish cleaning the apartment to turn in on that Saturday. Nevdra responded that she left the apartment key in the office, but lost the mailbox key, didn't have the gate opener, and still needed to hold on to the office key because she still hadn't had gotten a couple of the tables that she left in there after having weeks to do so with the excuse that it didn't fit in her car. This is the same car, by the way, where I had personally moved the furniture by myself in to the office so I know for sure that they fit. Nevdra then changed it to say that she couldn't pick them up by herself.

As for the address, Nevdra said that I didn't need to know it and asked me to clearly state why I needed it. Nevdra immediately said that I could send the divorce papers to her mother's address. That wasn't what I was thinking at the time, but I guess that Nevdra thought that's why I was needing her address and that's why she was hiding it from me because she thought that it would avoid a divorce. I was thinking that I would eventually need it for that reason, but it wasn't why I needed it then.

So why did I need her address then? For one thing, I wanted to send Necdra's mail directly to her because Nevdra had already accused me of stealing her Naturalization Certificate after she moved out because she couldn't find it. I had absolutely no idea where that was because the last time that I had seen it was in a grey box on a shelf at the top of our bedroom closet before she took all of her stuff from the closet. I guess that she found it because she didn't mention it again. But if anyone was going to steal it, my money would be on her little girlfriend Delia who was already working with fake or stolen papers so not a surprise if La Putina would take those. So, nope wasn't going to give her the chance to accuse me of stealing any of her mail by sending it to someone else's house.

Apparently, while we were texting back and forth, Nevdra had gone to the Police Department of the city where our apartment was to say that I was harassing her for her address. I found out because I received a phone call from a police officer while I was at work saying that he's with my wife and she says that I'm harassing her for her address and that I may try to accuse her of committing a crime against me. The officer also let me know that Nevdra had previously gone to them on that day when she moved all of her stuff out – yeah, when I was two hours away at work all day and barely speaking to her. I never knew that because the police officer was basically like "but he's two hours away, doesn't know that you're moving, and he's never given you any reason to think that he would do anything."

But for some reason, the police officer thought that he should contact me this time. Probably thought that Nevdra was pretty and wanted to suck up to her. Well, I had the time that day and was not having it! I told him why I wanted the address and he understood but was like *well if anything gets lost, it's not on you*. But I still laid into him to find out how in the world he could even fathom that I was harassing her. He thought that he was hot shit until I had him stuttering to respond. But since Nevdra had gotten the police involved, I asked the police why they weren't arresting her for all of the times that she had driven drunk. Hell, I'm sure that she even drove there not having *ever* had a driver's license. The officer said that he couldn't just take my word for it and thus couldn't arrest her since he didn't catch her in the act. Fair enough.

But Nevdra still had my keys. On that one, the officer saw something that he could do and got the keys from her. Oh, it also included the key that she had told me earlier that day that she had lost. Liar had it the whole time. I was still kind of livid, so I went full attorney mode on the officer and asked him why he was working with a known perpetrator of family violence against her victim – the time that Nevdra had gotten arrested for family violence was by the same police department that this officer was working for and she was taken to the same jail that was in the same building as his office. Guess that he forgot to look up if there were any cases between us because that would have shown up. He was again left stuttering trying to come up with an answer. Then it hit me… how the fuck does this officer even have any jurisdiction in this case?! Knowing Nevdra, I rightfully concluded that wherever she moved to wasn't in that city or even county. So neither Nevdra or I actually lived in that city where the police officer was and the text messages that were the basis of the "harassment" weren't made or received in that city either. At that point,

"Finish Him"[63] could have appeared above him because all he could do was admit that I was right and that he couldn't do anything even if he wanted to or there was something to do. Basically, all he could do was take an informational report and safeguard my keys until I could pick them up. I even think that he kept the keys so that I wouldn't feel like he completely wasted my time.

Looks like Nevdra was trying to "muddy the waters" by preempting me filing charges against her for family violence from when she broke my tooth. Like the *Saturday Night Live* skit said, "that's a bold move, let's see if it pays off for her." It didn't. *See*, I was still on the fence about whether I should file charges against her for breaking my tooth or not. Really, the only reason that I hadn't before was because she promised to stop drinking and get help for her alcoholism. If Nevdra had followed through with that, then I wouldn't have ever pressed charges against her even if we weren't together. Nevdra had paid the copay / deductible on the emergency dental repair and paid to fix my car, so if she had just gotten help to stop drinking and stuck with it, then that's all she would have had to do. As far as I was concerned, the relationship ended so if Nevdra had

---

[63] In the popular video game franchise of "Mortal Kombat", the words "Finish Him" would appear on screen when a character was defeated and the other character would have the opportunity to kill them off with a "Fatality" among other things.

not begged me to not end things, then the marriage would have stayed ended at that time. But Nevdra forced my hand because if I didn't file charges against her now, then I might lose my opportunity to do so later by her lying to the police before I could file those charges. It had only been a few months, and I had two years from when it happened to file charges so I was still thinking it over; but not anymore.

Nevdra probably thought that she was so clever going to the police, but she really screwed herself instead. First off, when Nevdra broke my tooth with the bottle, we both may have been living in the city and county where she tried to go to the police just now, but that happened in *another* city and county so she would have muddied the wrong waters. Second off, in looking up what charges Nevdra would face, I found another charge for *continuous family violence* that she could also be charged with for all of the times that she had physically assaulted me in our apartment and I could prove those with photos and videos. And lastly, Nevdra screwed herself by giving me her address indirectly anyways.

Remember that report that the police officer took because that's all he could do? Well, I ordered that report and Nevdra had given them an address that they included in the report. I will say that she was smart enough to not give the apartment number, but she did give the street address of the apartment complex. I would have NEVER have found that on my own. So with the apartment complex, it was only a matter of narrowing down which unit she was in.

Well, this is where I'm a little impressed with myself. Remember how Nevdra took almost all of the furniture and even the stuff that was mine? One of the things that Nevdra took was an egg-shaped patio swing. I had actually never seen her sit on it not once. As a matter of fact, only my daughters have ever sat in it. But Nevdra took it anyway. And even though I had blocked her, there were people who knew the situation who would send me the videos and pictures that she would post. And in one of those, that stupid egg chair was right there on her balcony. So, I figured that all I had to do was look for her car in the parking lot of the apartment complex to narrow down which building she was in and then look at the balconies for that piece of furniture. A good friend of mine offered to help me by looking for it. So I sent her a picture of Nevdra's car and the egg chair. My friend said that she found it the second that she turned into the apartment complex. She actually was disappointed by the lack of a challenge by how easy it was to find.

By the way, I never told Nevdra how I found her address. Nevdra even committed perjury in her criminal case by listing an address where she doesn't live on her bail / bond paperwork and by using that address every time that she signs a court form. So, I would have never found it had Nevdra not gone to the police to say that I was "harassing" her. If Nevdra ever reads this, guess that she'll now know how I got it. I actually told Nevdra that her friends would send me pictures and videos that she would upload on her social media and I got her address from the geo coordinates that were saved with those. As paranoid and distrusting as Nevdra is, I thought that it would be fun to get her to try to figure out which ones of her friends were betraying her. I was right because one of her friends did tell me that Nevdra called her pissed off accusing her of giving me information about her. Oh, I confirmed Nevdra's address by having her successfully personally served by the local constable with the divorce papers there.

Post Separation – Let the Healing Begin:

Breaking free from a narcissist is not an easy process. I read up a lot on the subject and the best advice is to cut off all communication with them because they crave attention – even negative attention. And giving them any attention just feeds them and keeps them going. They'll promise to change, offer you positive things, remind you of the good times, insult you, threaten you — basically do anything that they can think of to get you to engage with them. But you can't "feed their addiction", you have to cut them off, cut off their supply. And it was tempting, so tempting to fall into her trap. But fortunately, when Nevdra pulled her little stunt at the police station, it motivated me to stop talking to her. I only sent her one message after that and that was with the link to where I uploaded all of her pictures and videos from my phone.

Oh but it wasn't the same for Nevdra. She kept drunk texting and messaging me starting from the next day when she wrote "Robert. Por favor ya paremos con esto. Solo quiero pedirte perdón por no ser la mujer que tu necesitas. No somos enemigos.[64]" Nevdra probably knew that she messed up and wanted to do damage control on that one. And on August 23, 2024, starting at 3:17 AM until 9:49 AM she shared multiple TikTok videos, called several times, and sent and then immediately deleted a bunch of messages after sending them. In between all of those, she wrote "se que nunca lo miraras, pero eso no importa. Tu siempre estas en mi mente[65]" and other messages that I really couldn't comprehend because of how drunk Nevdra was when she wrote them. The parts that I could make out

---

[64] Translation: "Let's please stop with this. I just want to ask for your forgiveness for not being the woman that you need. We are not enemies"

[65] Translation: "I know that you'll never look at them, but it doesn't matter. You are always on my mind."

said that she loves me, a string of insults, and concludes with her saying that she regrets telling me that she still loves me. But then again on September 3, 2024 she wrote, "te extraño"[66].

But on October 5, 2024, Nevdra really tried to communicate with me; she actually called several times before finally texting: "Por qué haces eso mandarme las fotos en nuestro aniversario. Y al mismo tiempo pides el divorcio. No tiene sentido. Robert. Yo te amo. Te sigo amando solo di que tú me amas.[67]" That date *would* have been our 1st marriage anniversary. Guess that it technically still was since we were not divorced yet.

Well, before I had confirmed Nevdra's address, I created a photobook that told the entire story of our relationship from beginning to end and sent it to her daughter's apartment. I did that after I stopped speaking to Nevdra. It was a sort of catharsis as it was a way to literally close the book on our relationship. Since this happened after I stopped talking to her, I never knew if Nevdra had gotten it. Sure, the tracking said that it was delivered, but whether Jackie actually picked it up and/or gave it to her mother, I had no way of knowing.

---

[66] Translation: "I miss you"

[67] Translation: "Why do you do that [,] send the pictures on our wedding anniversary and at the same time ask for the divorce. It makes no sense. Robert, I love you and I keep loving you [,] just say that you love me."

Well, shortly after I had sent the photobook, I found some additional photos that I would have included if I had found them before. I also had some other minor changes that I wanted to make as well. After a few months, the website that I had done the photobook on had a promotion for unlimited additional pages on the photobook – just like when I did it the first time. Now that I had confirmed Nevdra's real address, I thought that I could perfect the photobook and make sure that Nevdra gets it this time. I hadn't planned this at all and the estimated date of delivery was supposed to be a few days *after* our anniversary, but it was delivered *early*. And Nevdra checked the mail that day. And that day coincidentally was our would-be first wedding anniversary date.

Not sure if my youngest daughter saw Nevdra's name come up on my phone when she was calling me, but she said that she hadn't seen Nevdra in a long time and missed her. That was unexpected. But on that day, I also knew that Nevdra was just talking and didn't actually still love me. Because if Nevdra had really loved me and wanted to be with me, then she would have made the drive to the apartment to apologize in person and ask for another chance. But she didn't… Nevdra actually posted a video of herself driving to the beach that day, so she clearly had the time to come had she really wanted to. And I don't think that Nevdra went to the beach that day so that no one could see her tears like how I had to take my daughters to the pool that day so that the water would wash away my tears without them knowing.

That was a rough day, like the day that I was driving with my two daughters when the youngest randomly said "I have 5 people in my family... me, [sister], daddy, and I have two moms – mommy and Elsa". She had never called Nevdra "mommy" before that and never even said anything like that before. That was probably around the same time that my mother called me and found out that Nevdra didn't join me in the move and that it was probably over. When my mom was confident enough that things were over, she let me have it. She basically chastised me for an hour over the phone. Yeah, all I could really do was take it because my mother was basically right about everything that she said. I do have to laugh a little because at one point my mother was like "well at least your Spanish improved and you lost a lot of weight, so she did do some good."

But it was rough, I had to start therapy to deal with it all and I did everything that I could think of to move on. I did the photo book, wrote her a final letter, sent her the last of her stuff that she never got, etc. Speaking of which, Nevdra didn't leave much, but she certainly didn't leave what she should have. Nevdra took all of the Christmas decorations including the ones that I had that were for my daughters (even ornaments that were pictures of them) and all of the keepsakes that I had of my daughters – birthday cards, Father's Day cards, drawings that they had made, etc. I get that they were mingled with her stuff, but she could have at least had the decency to mail them to me when she saw that she still had them. But she still *loves* me, right....

As the Frank Sinatra song's title suggests, "Love and Marriage" are two separate things. You can have one or the other, or both, or neither. So on November 4th, 2024, the Judge officially signed the Divorce Decree ending our brief, but eventful – *in a bad way* – marriage. I celebrated with a quiet dinner. There were a lot of mixed emotions. I felt mostly relief, but also disappointment that my marriage had failed and I was a three-time loser, and guilt that I had brought that woman into my daughters' lives. As for Nevdra, she wrote to me the next day on November 5, 2024, but all I saw was "This message was deleted". I think that Nevdra was under the common misconception among our people that she had to agree to the divorce and that I would have to talk to her to get her to sign the divorce decree. Hell no! If you get your spouse properly served and your spouse fails to respond (file an answer or otherwise appear in the divorce case), then you can default them after the default period ends. Some places also have a waiting period for divorces, but might be able to get those waived due to domestic violence (especially when there's a protective order) like I did. That was not even a consideration when I filed the criminal charges against her, but afterwards I realized that I could use it to not wait out the waiting period.

While on the subject, why did I file criminal charges against Nevdra? A few reasons actually, first and foremost there should be justice and no one should get away with a violent crime scot-free. Secondly, I am an attorney. So for better or worse, I have dedicated my life to the law and I should have confidence in it. Also, how can I look a client in the eyes and tell them that they should pursue a criminal case against someone when I myself didn't do it. As Doc Holliday said in the movie *Tombstone*, "my hypocrisy only goes so far." Thirdly, to actually save Nevdra's life. She may end up hating me, but at the rate that she was going, she was either going to hurt or kill herself or someone else – especially with all of the drunk driving that she does. And lastly, because I wanted to feel like I mattered. When the prosecutors picked up the charges and actually filed the case against her, it was empowering. After all of the times that I heard Nevdra downplaying what she did and telling me that it didn't matter, *it wasn't important* – it felt like I did matter, what happened to me mattered, it shouldn't have happened, and I mean something. That she's not going to get away with it just because she chose *me* as a victim.

You would think that the criminal case would have kept Nevdra from reaching out to me, but it didn't. Nevdra also signed up for a bunch of stuff and used my phone number so that they would contact me. How do I know that it was her? Well, they would use her name as the person who signed up who they were looking for. More brazen still, was on December 25, 2024, when Nevdra wrote: "Feliz Navidad mi amor[68]"– the real question is how did she meant it. Afterall, Christmas last year was when she hit me with the bottle. Was I supposed to read it as being genuine, threatening, or sarcastic? Text messages are fun that way as it really could be any of those three. But since the only person who could really tell me how it was meant was Nevdra, I guess that I'll never know.

After that, Nevdra only wrote me a few more times months apart. On February 25, 2025, Nevdra wrote "Robert". Again, not sure how I was supposed to interpret that. Guess that she was drunk and forgot to finish what she was going to write. The last message that I've received from her was on July 9, 2025 when she wrote: "Robert te escribe este mensaje

---

[68] Translation: "Merry Christmas, my love"

sabiendo que no debo, pero es algo que quiero hacer. Es de mi alma. De corazón. Solo quiero decirte que lo siento si hice algo que te lastimó. Hay veces no reaccione de la mejor manera. Te pido una vez más que me disculpes. Te pido perdón. De verdad Robert, jamás quise lastimarte. Y si lo hice, te juro no fue mi intención. Espero que algún día me perdones. Te quiero decir lo mucho que te."[69] Yeah, Nevdra's last sentence was incomplete so I don't know what she was trying to convey at the end.

Nevdralogue

Thank you for reading my story, I hope that it helped at least one person. I actually started writing this because one of the people who helped me get through this – I couldn't have done it without her love and support – encouraged me to write about my experience after I told her that I couldn't find any books from a man who was the victim of domestic violence by a woman. Originally, I thought that I could use my experience to do stand-up comedy as I use comedy to deal with trauma and all this trauma made me hilarious. If you haven't noticed this, the clown is funny

---

[69] Translation: "Robert, I write this message knowing that I shouldn't, but it's something that I want to do. This is from my soul. My heart. I just want to tell you that I'm sorry if I did something to hurt you. There are times when I don't react in the best way. I ask you again to forgive me. I ask for your forgiveness. For real Robert, I never wanted to hurt you. And if I did it, I swear that it wasn't my intention. I hope that one day you will forgive me. I want to tell you how much I ... you (incomplete sentence)."

because they use comedy to mask their pain and cope with trauma. To quote Friedrich Nietzsche, "man alone suffers so excruciatingly in the world that he was compelled to invent laughter." But she convinced me that a book might actually help people that were going through a similar situation as a book she read once helped her leave an abusive ex once.

And it will be rough. Every time I look in the mirror, I see the scars on my body that I didn't have before our relationship. I had gotten a tattoo as part of the healing process, and my mother thought that I had gotten more than one and misunderstood when she was told that I got one on my back. That mark wasn't a tattoo, it was a scar that Nevdra had left on me. Not a pleasant moment...

So here's my advice: you may think that you're alone in this and no one else has dealt with this, but you're wrong. You're not the only one that this has happened to. Society expects men to "suffer in silence" but you don't need to suffer in silence, you're a human being and your suffering is genuine and matters. Men can be victims and women can be the abuser. And more importantly, there are always people willing to listen and even help. You just have to look. Part of what a narcissist does is isolate you from people so that you feel like there's no one there to help you, and you have to rely on her – even taking the abuse. But don't be afraid to reach out to people that you were isolated from out of shame, pride, etc. And yes, not everyone wants to get involved and not everyone is a good person. When you're at your lowest, you'll never forget two people: those who took advantage of you and those that helped you. This is when you'll find out who is a true friend and who isn't.

As for Nevdra, "se dice que por cada hombre, hay una como tú[70]…" But after a criminal case that lasted over a year, she took a "sweetheart deal" where she would do a 13-month *pre-trial intervention* that would involve the completion of domestic violence classes, treatment, programs, and no alcohol. Not very confident that she can go 13 months without alcohol, but guess that we will see...

---

[70] Translation "it is said that for every man, there is one like you", a line from the song "Mi Historia Entre Tus Dedos" by Gianluca Grignani

Amar a una Alcohólica... ("La Otra")

Estoy enamorado de ti. Amo a la persona quien eres: tu mente, cuerpo y alma. ¡Eres perfecta! Así que me rompe el corazón verte convertirte en otra persona; alguien que no es la mujer que amo. Y no entiendo por qué querrías convertirte en "La Otra", la que temo; la que me lastima.

Cada vez que sales, tengo esa sensación en la boca del estómago que desearía nunca haber sentido y desearía no volver a sentir de nuevo. Se siente como un vacío, un hueco, que está esperando de hacer llenado con algo terrible. Existe el temor de que vayas a beber y regreses a casa como "La Otra". Pero siempre hay una pequeña esperanza de que esta vez – esta vez – sea diferente; que vas a rechazar la bebida y volver a casa normal. Desafortunadamente, sé que no es así y terminó desilusionado y decepcionado. Espero no tener que prepararme para cuando vuelva. Pero no eres tú quien regresa, es "La Otra". Y tengo que prepararme para la llegada de "La Otra": poner las llaves y la cartera en algún lugar que pueda agarrar rápidamente junto con la ropa en caso de que tenga que salir con solo unos segundos de sobra, cerrar las puertas con llave y esconder las cosas en la habitación en caso de que tenga que esconderme de ti, y mover las cosas fuera de la vista para que no las rompas o tírame las.

¿Y quién es "La Otra"? Es quien se parece a ti, pero arrastra las palabras, tropieza cuando camina, escucha cosas que nunca se dijeron, tiene un aliento que apesta a alcohol y tiene "la mirada", una mirada en blanco que no tiene alma detrás. "La Otra" es peligrosa. Ella es violenta e hiriente, rencorosa e irrazonable. Dice las cosas más viles y dolorosas con pura malicia; incluso si es todo lo contrario de lo que has dicho, "La Otra" lo dirá con tal convicción que es completamente creíble – ella dice cosas que me romperán el corazón sin hesitación. Ella me acusa de todo con todo el mundo sin ninguna evidencia o motivo y no escuchará nada de lo que diga ni mirará ninguna evidencia que contradiga su delirio. "La Otra" no solo me atacará con sus palabras, sino también físicamente. Me tirará cosas, intentará estrangularme con un cable de carga, me apuñalará con un tenedor, me arranca la ropa mientras la llevo puesta, me abofetea, me patea, me arañará, clavará sus uñas en mi carne, rompe mi diente con una botella, y hasta intenta hacernos chocar. Y lo peor de todo, ni siquiera recuerda lo que hizo o dijo. Si no fuera por las cosas dañadas, los vidrios rotos, la buena comida tirada a la basura, los arrestos, los casos judiciales, las bocas ensangrentadas, los trabajos dentales de emergencia, las publicaciones vergonzosas, y los mensajes incoherentes, ni siquiera creerías lo que hiciste.

Pero, de lejos, lo más doloroso que hace "La Otra" es hacerme cuestionar "por qué". ¿Por qué quieres hacerme daño? ¿Por qué quieres decirme las cosas más hirientes que se te ocurran? ¿Por qué quieres cicatrizarme y desfigurarme? ¿Por qué quieres dañar nuestra relación? ¿Qué te hice yo que fue tan malo para hacerme merecer esto? Y el mayor "por qué" es ¿por qué bebes tanto? ¿Por qué hay que beber hasta el punto de que aparezca "La Otra"? ¿Por qué no puedes dejar de beber antes de eso? ¿Por qué tienes que aceptar una bebida cuando te la ofrecen? ¿Por qué empiezas a beber? ¿Qué ganas con esto? Con tanto que has perdido y podrías perder, ¿qué hace que la "recompensa" valga la pena el "riesgo"? Antes de empezar a beber, antes de abrir la botella, antes de comprar o aceptar la botella, ¿piensas en mí? ¿Cruzo tu mente en ningún momento? No puedo evitar preguntarme...

¿Alguna vez te dirás a ti mismo: "sabes que, realmente no vale la pena" antes de comenzar a beber? ¿Alguna vez aprenderás a lidiar con la adversidad en lugar de correr hacia una botella al más mínimo problema?

Después de que las cosas se han puesto realmente mal unas cuantas veces, has admitido que tienes un problema e incluso has pedido ayuda. Pero cuando te lo he ofrecido, no lo has cumplido. Y luego prometiste que dejarías de beber, pero no lo hiciste. Me pediste perdón, pero solo con palabras vacías y no con acciones. Realmente amo a la persona quién eres, pero odio "La Otra" en la que te transformas cuando bebes. Espero que llegue un día en que "La Otra" desaparezca para siempre. Sé que es difícil cambiar y que no puedes hacerlo solo. Solo puedo esperar y rezar para que algún día busques la ayuda que necesitas, qué es lo único que no puedo hacer por ti, pero que tienes que hacer por ti mismo.

To Love an Alcoholic... (a.k.a. The Other)

I am in love with you. I love the person who you are: your mind, body, and soul. You are perfect! So, it breaks my heart to see you become someone else; someone who is not the woman that I love. And I don't understand why you'd want to become "the other", the one that I fear; the one that hurts me.

Every time you go out, I get that feeling in the pit of my stomach that I wish I would have never felt and wish that I'd never feel again. It feels like an emptiness, a hole that is waiting to get filled with something terrible. There's a fear that you will go drink and come back home as "the other." But there is always a small hope that this time – this one time – will be different; that you'll turn down the drink and just come home normal. Unfortunately, I know better and end up disillusioned and disappointed. I hope that I don't have to prepare myself for when you return. But it is not you who returns – it is "the other." And I do have to prepare for "the other's" arrival: put my keys and wallet somewhere that I can grab quickly along with clothes in case I have to leave with only a few seconds to spare, pre-lock doors and hide things in the room in case I have to hide myself from you, and move things out of view so that you won't break them or throw them at me.

And who is "the other"? It's who looks like you, but slurs her words, stumbles when she walks, hears things that were never said, has a breath that reeks of alcohol, and has "the look" – a blank stare that has no soul behind it. "The other" is dangerous. She is violent and hurtful, spiteful, and unreasonable. She says the most vile and painful things with pure malice; even if it's the complete opposite of what you've said, "the other" will say it with such conviction that it is completely believable – she will say things that break my heart without any hesitation. She will accuse me of everything with everyone without any evidence or even motive and won't listen to anything that I say or look at any evidence that contradicts her delusion. "The other" will not only attack me with her words, but physically as well. She will throw things at me, try to choke me with a charging cable, stab me with a fork, rip my clothes while I'm wearing them, slap me, kick me, scratch me, dig her nails into my flesh, break my tooth with a bottle, and even try to make us crash. And worse of all, she won't even remember what she did or said. If it weren't for the damaged things, the broken glass, the good food thrown in the trash, the arrest, court cases, the bloody mouths, emergency dental work, the embarrassing posts, and the incoherent messages, you wouldn't even believe what you did.

But, by far, the most hurtful thing that "the other" does is make me question "why". Why do you want to hurt me? Why do you want to say the most hurtful things that you can think of to me? Why do you want to scar and disfigure me? Why do you want to damage our relationship? What did I do to you that was so wrong to make me deserve this? And the biggest "why" is why do you drink so much at all? Why must you drink to the point that "the other" appears? Why can't you stop drinking before that? Why must you accept a drink when it's offered to you? Why do you even start drinking? What do you gain from this? With so much that you have lost and could lose, what makes the "reward" worth the "risk"? Before you start drinking, before you open the bottle, before you buy or accept the bottle, do you think about me? Do I cross your mind at all? I can't help but wonder…

Will you ever say to yourself, "you know, it's really not worth it" before you start drinking? Will you ever learn to deal with adversity instead of running to a bottle at the slightest problem?

After things have gotten really bad a few times, you have admitted that you have a problem and even asked for help. But when I have offered it to you, you haven't followed through on it. And then you promised that you'd stop drinking, but you didn't. You asked me for forgiveness, but only with hollow words and not with any actions. I really love the person who you are, but I hate "the other" who you transform into when you drink. I hope that there can come a day when "the other will disappear forever. I know that it is difficult to change and that you can't do it alone. I can just hope and pray that you one day will seek the help that you need – which is the one thing that I can't do for you, but you have to do for yourself.